Parenting

BABY MUST-HAVES

Parenting

BABY

MUST-

HAVES

Time Inc.
HOME ENTERTAINMENT

Publisher Richard Fraiman
General Manager Steven Sandonato
Executive Director, Marketing Services Carol Pittard
Director, Retail & Special Sales Tom Mifsud
Director, New Product Development Peter Harper
Assistant Director, Brand Marketing Laura Adam
Assistant General Counsel Dasha Smith Dwin
Book Production Manager Suzanne Janso
Design & Prepress Manager Anne-Michelle Gallero
Marketing Manager Alexandra Bliss

Special Thanks Bozena Bannett, Glenn Buonocore,
Robert Marasco, Jonathan Polsky, Brooke Reger,
Mary Sarro-Waite, Ilene Schreider, Adriana Tierno,
Alex Voznesenskiy

Copyright 2007
Time Inc. Home Entertainment

Time Inc.
1271 Avenue of the Americas
New York, New York 10020

ISBN 13: 978-1-933821-11-5
ISBN 10: 1-933821-11-6
Library of Congress #: 2007903236

We welcome your comments and suggestions
about our books. Please write to us at:
Parenting Magazine's *Baby Must-Haves*
Attention: Book Editors
PO Box 11016
Des Moines, IA 50336-1016

If you would like to order any of our hardcover
Collector's Edition books, please call us at
1-800-327-6388. (Monday through Friday,
7:00 a.m.–8:00 p.m. or Satuday, 7:00 a.m.–
6:00 p.m. Central Time).

Parenting
magazine

Editor-in-Chief Janet Chan
Executive Editor Lisa Bain
Art Director Kayo Der Sarkissian
Deputy Editor Ellen Fair
Assistant Managing Editor Gina E. Grant
Research Director Ann Sackrider
Contributing Editor Maura Rhodes

President, Group Publisher
Jeff Wellington
General Manager Beverly Ivens
Group Associate Publisher, Marketing
Marnie Lefcoe Braverman
Consumer Marketing Director
Nicole Martel Banas
**Associate Director, PR and
Communications** Catherine McManus

DOWNTOWN
BOOKWORKS INC.

President Julie Merberg
Editors Sara Newberry, Sarah Parvis
Assistant Editor Kate Gibson
Designer Jill Armus
Production Designer Jon Glick
Special Thanks Patty Brown, Pam Abrams

HAVING A BABY means turning your life upside down in (mostly) wonderful ways. While it's nearly impossible to prepare for the emotional upheaval, you *can* arm yourself for the practical aspects of being a mom.

There are tons of products out there to help keep your baby warm and dry, happy and healthy, well fed, and well rested. But how do you know what to choose?

That's why we decided to pool all of our resources—including our staffers and moms across the country—to create Parenting *magazine's Baby Must-Haves.* This guide will direct you to the products that you really need: the can't-live-withouts, the lifesavers, the items that are ideally suited to your family and your circumstances.

How did we decide which products made the cut? At *Parenting* magazine, we've been talking to moms for more than 20 years. Our editors are tuned in to moms' needs—over 11 million readers turn to us every month! We've also cultivated a team of hundreds of volunteer moms across the country who reality-test products with their own families. When they report back on their favorites, we know these products have been approved by the toughest critics out there: moms like you.

And we invited moms to participate in a national survey—more than 1,200 responded to questions on *Parenting*'s MomConnection.com about which products and brands they loved (or didn't), which features were important (or weren't), and why. They also shared great tips on everything from where and when to find the best bargains to surprising items that will lull any baby to sleep. You'll find these priceless "Mom Tips!" throughout the book.

The collective wisdom and experience of our family of editors and moms is organized here to make your life a little simpler. Taking this book with you when you shop is like having hundreds of moms who've already been down that aisle steering your cart and whispering in your ear. As well as saving you some money (Skip the baby carriage! Borrow a bassinet!), our guide will help you save time, so you'll have more time to just enjoy your baby.

We double-checked our facts, but bear in mind that specific models may be discontinued or change slightly from year to year. The red stroller you see pictured may only come in green stripes, or might have a bigger basket by the time you're ready to buy. Prices vary from store to store, and from year to year, as well. But the brands we recommend have proven reliable again and again, so chances are, the next generation of a particular model will satisfy as well as the current one does.

Also, there's a steady stream of new products hitting the market that may not have been available when this book went to press. Check in at parenting. com for news on any exciting new items or product recalls. And please e-mail me at **janet@parenting.com** if you discover more must-haves—we'll pass them along to other moms on our site and in the next edition of this book. We look forward to hearing from you!

JANET CHAN
Editor-in-Chief, *Parenting* magazine

5

INTRODUCTION

CONTENTS

1 THE NURSERY

BABIES spend about two-thirds of their time snoozing, so most won't notice or even care where they're napping, at least for the first year or so. But *you* will. Even if you plan to have the baby sleep in your room in the early months, or simply put a used crib in a corner of the guest room (more about hand-me-down furniture on page 15), it's likely you'll do an about-face once you start flipping through catalogs or wandering through stores.

Your baby's nursery can be frilly and old-fashioned or sleek and modern, pastel and calming or brightly colored and stimulating. It can feature creatures from dragons to dragonflies or characters from ballerinas to cowboys. Whatever you choose, your child's room should contain several essential elements:

A place for the baby to sleep Some newborns sleep in cribs in their own rooms from day one; others spend the first weeks sleeping in their parents' bedrooms, preferably in a bassinet or a co-sleeper (a baby bed that attaches to your bed). Where your baby sleeps depends on whether you nurse (if so, having him close will make wee-hour feedings much easier), and whether you're a light sleeper (newborns can be noisy nappers).

A place for diaper changing You don't need to have a changing table, but it will make life easier. You can also buy a changing table that "grows up" to be a regular dresser that your child can use for years. (For more on converting a regular dresser into a changing table, see page 29.)

A place for cuddling and feeding As a cozy place to nurse or give your baby a bottle or kick up your feet while you're calming him down, a glider or rocking chair can be an invaluable investment. As your baby gets older, it will be a favorite spot for snuggling and storytime.

A way to keep tabs on her while you're out of the room In most homes—especially if you close the door to the nursery—you may not be able to hear your baby crying when she wakes up. This is where a baby monitor comes in.

Beyond these essentials, there are plenty of items you'll want or need for your baby's room. Read on to learn more about choosing—and using—it all.

9

BASSINETS & CRADLES

MANY NEW BABIES spend their first three months or so sleeping in one of these cozy contraptions, most of which are roughly a third the size of a regular crib. To a baby fresh from the confines of the womb, the enclosed space will feel comforting. For a weary mom or dad, starting out with a baby bed that's small enough to fit into the master bedroom can save many precious steps and minutes when a wailing baby needs tending to in the middle of the night.

Also in this category of first beds are Moses baskets, which are admittedly quaint and low-tech but not very practical, given that they essentially mean parking your baby on the floor, where she'll be less accessible to you but easily reached by the dog, your jealous toddler, or the dust you haven't had time to vacuum since giving birth. One apartment-dwelling mom in our survey, though, loved the Moses basket because of its compact size. And, she said, "I'll either use it for my next child—or as a toy basket."

How bassinets and cradles stack up:

BASSINETS

Strictly speaking, a bassinet is a newborn baby bed. Many of them feature an attached, half-dome-shaped canopy at one end to help block light from a sleeping baby's eyes and also contribute to the bassinet's snuggly feel. Some models have an open shelf underneath for storage. Others are more like a big basket.

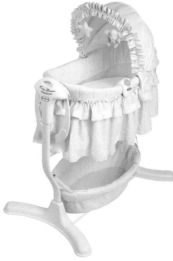

◄ KOLCRAFT'S CONTOURS COZY DREAMS GLIDING BASSINET (ABOUT $150) HAS A TIMER, SO YOU DON'T HAVE TO WORRY ABOUT TURNING IT OFF AFTER YOUR BABY HAS FALLEN ASLEEP.

Mom Tip!

"Look for a bassinet with wheels. Even though my newborn spent most of the time sleeping, I liked being able to wheel her around from room to room so I could keep an eye on her without disturbing her."

Many are on wheels—earning them points for portability. Style-wise, they tend to be on the froufrou side, with ruffles or pleats of fabric (from white eyelet to pink or blue prints and everything in between) adorning the outside and fringing the canopy. Some super-fancy styles are round and sport more traditional, draping types of canopies. That said, plainer versions can be found if you're a no-frills kind of person.

Most bassinets are sold with a "mattress"— typically a one-inch-thick vinyl pad—for which you can buy fitted sheets; some are also padded on the inside. If the interior of the bassinet is not padded, you can get a dust ruffle that both pads the interior of the basket and then drapes over the exterior and down to the floor.

▲ EXTRA STORAGE, LIKE THE SHELF ON THIS EDDIE BAUER BASSINET (ABOUT $140), ALWAYS COMES IN HANDY FOR BURP CLOTHS, WIPES, DIAPERS, AND MORE.

CRADLES

These rocking beds come in two versions: Either the bed part is mounted directly on rockers, or it's mounted on a frame so that the bed rocks independently. Often, cradles constructed in this way are on casters, so they can be moved about easily.

In both cases, the rocking motion is from side to side, which is one thing to consider when baby-bed shopping; sideways isn't always the most soothing motion for a baby. Studies have shown most infants prefer to move forward and back (as a rocking chair does), as this more closely mimics the motion they enjoyed for the nine months they spent in the womb.

Cradles tend to be considerably less ornate than bassinets; many resemble mini cribs, with natural or painted wooden slats. But you can find fancier ones, made of wicker, for example, or with spindly rails. Mattresses are usually included. Underbed storage isn't an option.

11

Sleep position-
ers are foam
cushions that
are marketed
as tools to keep
your infant safe
on her back.
Don't bother
with them! It's
much safer to
keep the crib
free of clutter
(no quilts,
stuffed animals,
or pillows),
according to
child safety
experts.

THINGS TO CONSIDER:

◆ **Lifespan** Most bassinets and cradles will accommodate babies only for the first three months or so. (A squirmy
baby may outgrow her bassinet even sooner.) Be sure to
check the age and weight recommendations on whatever
product you're about to buy.

◆ **Durability** Look for a bassinet or cradle with solid
construction and a wide, stable base.

◆ **Safety** Make sure that the mattress (and any padding) is
smooth and fits snugly, and test the width of the slats; they
shouldn't be wide enough for a baby's head to fit through.
(See guide to buying cribs on pages 14–16 for specific
measurements.) Don't pile on the bedding; extra blankets,
soft toys, and the like are all suffocation hazards for an
infant who's too young to turn his head away if something
inadvertently covers his face. (This goes for anywhere a
baby sleeps.) Be aware, too, that any baby who's able
to sit up or roll over shouldn't be in a bassinet or cradle,
because she could easily tumble out of it.

◆ **Extras** Many bassinets (less so cradles) feature all sorts
of add-ons designed to make your life easier and/or your
baby's more pleasant. Some play music, vibrate, convert
to rockers (which effectively turn them into bassinet/
cradle hybrids), have a light to help mom or dad see
what's going on in the middle of the night,
or can be used as changing
tables once they're out-
grown. As with anything,
expect to pay more for
such perks: A basic bas-
sinet can be had for as
little as $50; an elaborate
model might set you
back $150 or more.

◄ THIS WICKER
BASSINET FROM
L.A. BABY (ABOUT
$99) LIFTS OFF OF
ITS WHEELED BASE
SO YOU CAN TAKE
THE BASKET FROM
ROOM TO ROOM.

▲ SMALLER THAN STANDARD CO-SLEEPERS, THE ARM'S REACH MINI CO-SLEEPER (ABOUT $190) IS IDEAL FOR BEDROOMS THAT DON'T HAVE A LOT OF SPACE TO SPARE.

A RELATIVE NEWCOMER to the baby-bed bunch, a co-sleeper is essentially a three-sided bassinet that attaches to a regular bed. It can be the answer for a nursing mom who would love to tuck her baby in next to her at night in order to make feedings easier—but knows this is neither safe nor practical. (It's hard to sleep well when there's seven pounds of precious cargo in your bed.)

The original co-sleeper manufacturer, **Arm's Reach,** still makes the majority of these beds, but since they were introduced, the company has come out with various options, including a mini version for smaller bedrooms (about $130) and a sleigh bed style ($309). The original model runs about $191; except for the sleigh bed style, all can be converted into a play yard. All models can be used as regular, four-sided baby beds and have storage space underneath. You can get more information about these at armsreach.com.

When using a co-sleeper, make sure that it fits snugly against the big bed it's attached to, so there's no space for a baby to roll into and get trapped. Keep bedding simple (no loose blankets, no plush toys). Once your child can sit up or roll over, switch her to a crib—as with bassinets and cradles, co-sleepers aren't deep enough to keep a mobile baby safe.

CRIBS

YOUR BABY'S CRIB should be a safe haven—a place where she can sleep or play comfortably, without any danger of getting hurt.

When choosing a crib, be sure to look for:

◆ **Screws, brackets, and joints** that are tightly in place and intact. (Obviously, if you assemble the crib yourself, make sure you screw and tighten all the parts correctly.)

◆ **A mattress** that fits snugly, so your baby can't slip down between it and the crib frame and become trapped. Note that most mattresses are sold separately from the crib.

◆ **Slats** that are no more than $2^3/8$ inches apart. If you can slip a soda can between the slats, they're wide enough for your baby's head to fit through and get stuck.

◆ **Corner posts** that don't extend more than $1/16$ inch, so that your child's clothing can't get snagged on them.

◆ **A headboard and footboard without decorative cut-outs** that your baby could trap her head in.

◆ **Adjustable mattress levels** so that as your baby learns how to sit, stand, and then climb, you can lower the mattress. (Most cribs can be adjusted to at least two different mattress levels.)

◆ **Rolling casters,** to make it easier to move the crib around the nursery.

◆ **At least one drop side,** so that it's easier to put your newborn down on the mattress. Two drop sides make for more flexible positioning in the nursery. The drop side should have a locking mechanism so that the baby can't release it.

NOTE: Make sure that any new crib you're considering is approved by the Consumer Product Safety Commission (CPSC). Log on to cpsc.gov to search for product recalls and find out about product safety standards.

▲ A SLEIGH CRIB CAN BE A CLASSY ADDITION TO A SPACIOUS NURSERY.

▲ IKEA'S HENSVIK SPINDLE CRIB ($129) IS ABOUT AS BASIC AS THEY COME.

Mom Tip!

"In the store, see if you can lower the crib rail with one hand (which you'll need to do if you're holding your baby). And make sure it raises and lowers silently so you'll be able to move it without waking a sleeping baby!"

Mom Tip!

"I put a heating pad in my baby's crib to warm it up (and remove it, of course, before putting her down to sleep)."

GIZMOS & GADGETS

Teething rails are strips of soft rubber that clip or adhere onto the top horizontal rail of a crib—often viewed as a delicacy by teething babies looking for something hard to chew on. They aren't necessary—gnawing on her crib won't hurt your baby, but she might enjoy the "chewier" surface of the rubber, and once a few of her chompers are fully in, the rail might help protect the crib's finish from toothmarks, especially if it's painted. One option: **Gummi Crib Rails** ($14; onestepahead.com): At 50 inches long, they can be cut to size if necessary

You can spend anywhere from $100 to over $1,000 on a crib. The more expensive models, in addition to having more features (like the capacity to convert into something else, or storage drawers), are usually made of sturdier materials: high-quality wood, as opposed to laminates. More intricate designs or handwork may also account for higher price tags.

▲ THE SIMPLE DESIGN OF POTTERY BARN'S KENDALL CRIB ($599) WILL COORDINATE WITH LOTS OF DECORATING STYLES.

$KIP, $AVE, OR $PLURGE?

If you're thinking of buying or borrowing a used crib, look it over carefully to make sure it's up to snuff. If you determine that it was manufactured prior to 1990, skip it, buy new, and save the bucks elsewhere: Older-model cribs cause more than 9,000 injuries and up to 50 deaths every year. There are plenty of affordable new models. If you're buying for a first baby and planning to have more, this is a good place to splurge on something sturdy and beautiful. One mom in our survey raved about the durability of her **Babee Tenda Crib** (babeetenda.com): "I've had five children, and the crib is just as sturdy for my fifth child as it was for the first." Always buy a new mattress.

THE CHOICES:

Now comes the fun part—picking a style that you like. Start by figuring out what kind of crib you need, then think about the finish—whether you want natural or painted wood.

STANDARD MODELS come in several styles (Jenny Lind cribs with spindles and sleigh cribs are very popular). If you expect to have more kids, it's a good idea to stick with a standard model so your first will move into a toddler or twin bed when baby No. 2 is ready for the crib.

CONVERTIBLE CRIBS most often convert to toddler beds. Some convert further, to a twin bed, daybed, or love seat. Convertible cribs make sense if this is your only (or last) child, provided you find a sturdy model that can survive all of these stages. They're slightly more expensive (though you do get a lot of bang for the buck), and the conversion kits are almost always sold separately.

CANOPY CRIBS come with a fabric canopy—strictly an aesthetic decision. Some people like to match the canopy material to the nursery.

ROUND CRIBS require round mattresses and tend to be more expensive than standard models.

MINI CRIBS are designed for small spaces, and many models are portable.

Mom Tip!
(for multiples)

"When I had twins I bought one really good crib first to share until they were rolling over. That gave me time to save up for a second nice crib."

Mom Tip!

"The best thing I bought was a convertible crib. It made the transition from crib to toddler bed much easier."

▲ A CRIB THAT CONVERTS TO A TODDLER BED OR DAYBED CAN TAKE YOUR CHILD ALL THE WAY TO KINDERGARTEN.

GIZMOS & GADGETS

Lots of moms in our survey said that some sort of sound machine was a must-have in the nursery. Several popular options are available at **sleep-wellbaby.com,** including the **Marpac Sleep Mate Sound Conditioner** ($43), which creates "white noise," and the **BebeSounds Nursery Air Purifier** ($40), which not only drowns out sounds but also filters dust and allergens from the air. (Just remember: You don't want your baby to get too used to sleeping in total quiet. She needs to be able to snooze through the sound of the vacuum cleaner and other normal noises so that she can nap no matter where she is or what's going on.)

► FISHER PRICE'S FLUTTERBYE MOBILE ($35) MOVES AND GROOVES.

BABIES SPEND A LOT of time in their cribs and not all of it sleeping. While we cover toys extensively in Chapter 11, the one "must-have" for crib entertainment is a mobile.

Look for:

◆ Bold patterns and bright, contrasting colors (not necessarily black-and-white).

◆ Images that face the baby, not outward.

◆ If you like, a mobile that plays music or revolves. Avoid flashing lights; these could make it hard for your baby to drift off to sleep.

◆ A way to connect the mobile to the crib that's secure and stable, such as with clamps, Velcro, or double-knotted ties.

◆ Strings that are no longer than 6 inches.

◆ No sharp edges or small parts that could break off and make their way into your baby's mouth.

NOTE: Remove the mobile from the crib as soon as your baby can push up on his hands and knees—since at that stage, he could easily reach it and pull it down.

Mom Tip!

"An exercise ball turned out to be my best purchase. I got it originally hoping it would help me to lose my pregnancy weight. Then I discovered that gently bouncing on it while holding my baby actually lulled her to sleep."

17

SOME OPTIONS:

Most companies that make infant toys make mobiles (some bouncy seats and play yards are equipped with them). A few favorites include the **Dreams in Sight mobile** ($40; **The First Years**), which not only plays different tunes (and comes with a remote so that you can be the DJ from across the room), but also has a night-light; and **Fisher-Price's Flutter-bye Dreams Lullaby Birdies mobile** ($35). Moms also like the **Symphony in Motion Mobile** (about $40; **Tiny Love**).

An alternative to a mobile is a toy that attaches to the side of the crib. One that gets repeated raves is the **Ocean Wonders Aquarium**, by **Fisher-Price** ($30). This toy resembles a small TV screen on which sea creatures swim calmly in sync with mesmerizing aquatic sounds and music. "Our son loved it, especially when the lights shone on the ceiling and he could see a mini movie of the fish swimming," reported one mom; another said that her 3-year-old still uses hers to get to sleep.

▲ A LIGHTS-OUT SOOTHER: THE DREAMS IN SIGHT MOBILE ($40) PROJECTS STARS AND MOONS ONTO THE CEILING ABOVE THE CRIB.

▲ THE SYMPHONY IN MOTION MOBILE (ABOUT $40) HAS SEVERAL CLASSICAL TUNES TO CHOOSE FROM.

▼ FOR MANY MOMS, THE FISHER-PRICE OCEAN WONDERS AQUARIUM ($30) IS DREAMY!

IT'S TIME for your child to move out of her crib when:
- ◆ **She's 35 inches tall** or the top of the side rail is below mid-chest level.
- ◆ **She's running out of room** to roll over or bumping her arms and legs against the sides of her crib as she sleeps.
- ◆ **She's climbing out**—or trying mighty hard to.

And when that day comes, you have a number of options. Some parents simply make up a mattress on the floor; others install a guard rail on the side of a regular bed. If the former option feels too messy, and the latter is impractical (your child's room is too small for a larger bed) or unappealing (you're not quite ready yourself to put your growing-up-too-fast baby in a regular bed), and if you'd like your child to feel like she's moving to a space that's all hers, consider investing in a toddler bed.

Toddler beds typically accommodate standard crib mattresses, making them the perfect transitional bed for kids who might be overwhelmed by the expanse of a regular bed.

For parental peace of mind, most toddler beds come with guardrails on both sides; often these rails are slatted (like those on a crib), and extend about a third of the way down from the head of the bed to allow easy access at tuck-in time. Some guardrails can be detached. Toddler beds are also low to the ground, making it safe for a toddler to climb in and out "all by myself!"

▼ CREATURE COMFORT: IKEA'S KRITTER BED ($70) HAS A BUILT-IN GUARDRAIL.

▲ LAND OF NOD'S STORAGE BED HAS DRAWERS THAT MAKE PRE-BEDTIME TOY PICKUPS EASIER (FROM $499–$899).

WHEN CHOOSING A TODDLER BED:

◆ Make sure that it's sturdy and of solid construction.

◆ Check to see that any hardware is positioned where it can't poke a sleeping child.

◆ Look out for small parts that could break off and pose a choking hazard to a very young toddler who may be compelled to put stuff into her mouth.

◆ Feel between the mattress and frame to make sure that the mattress fits snugly on all four sides.

◆ As with other types of children's furniture, consider only a toddler bed that's CPSC-approved.

The big difference between buying the two types of beds, though, is that cribs are designed to appeal to the parents' aesthetics, while many toddler beds are designed to appeal to increasingly self-aware tots—in other words, kids who've developed specific interests (aka "obsessions") in any manner of thing, from fire trucks to SpongeBob.

If catering to your child's cartoonish inclinations doesn't appeal to you, though, there are plenty of toddler beds that resemble scaled-down versions of grown-up ones, including sleigh beds, white painted "Nantucket-style" versions trimmed in wainscoting, and sophisticated styles stained in ebony. A handful of beds even feature a trundle drawer underneath for storage. Prices range from as little as $40 for a molded-plastic, character-themed bed to $100 or more for a solid-wood, traditional style. You can save on bedding by simply using the sheets from your child's crib.

GIZMOS & GADGETS

You can skip the toddler bed altogether and go straight to a twin bed by outfitting it with a guard rail, like **Summer Infant's Sure and Secure Double** and **Triple Bedrails.** The triple protects the head of the bed as well as the sides ($35 for the double, $50 for the triple; summerinfant.com). Another option: the **BedBugz Bed Bolster,** a soft inflatable tube bedecked with cute little bugs that attaches to the side of the bed ($40; toddlercoddler.com).

21

BEDDING

◄ BABYLICIOUS MAKES BLANKETS AND BEDDING SETS (INCLUDING A QUILT, BUMPER PAD, CRIB SKIRT, AND FITTED CRIB SHEET) TO MATCH JUST ABOUT ANY DÉCOR ($26).

YOUR BABY WILL BE PERFECTLY HAPPY to snooze on a plain white cotton sheet, swaddled in the same frowsy flannel blanket the nurses wrapped him in at the hospital. But chances are, once you've chosen a crib, you're going to want to dress it up.

There are hundreds of baby bedding options, including sheets, blankets, quilts, bumpers (padded panels that wrap around the inside of the crib), and crib skirts that can all be bought separately. You can also buy complete bedding sets that typically include a sheet, bumper, quilt, and skirt (often with coordinating pillows and window treatments). How you choose to make your baby's bed—à la carte or prix fixe—depends on your own decorating style. If you like to mix and match different patterns, colors, and fabrics, there are plenty of separates out there to play with. Ditto if you prefer to buy pieces that already go together.

Ultimately the choices you make for crib bedding will depend on these factors, not necessarily in this order: your taste, your budget, and your baby's gender. If your idea of the perfect crib is one outfitted in eyelet and lace, you can find it. Love the idea of surrounding your child with images of storybook characters? There are lots of options for you. Color choices are endless—from soothing pastels to cheery primaries to sophisticated combos like brown and

GIZMOS & GADGETS

If you're worried that your baby's crib sheets aren't fitting properly, you can buy some extra peace of mind with clips designed to hold the corners taut. **Safety 1st** sells **Crib Sheet Security Clips** in packs of four for $4 (safety1st.com).

$KIP, $AVE, OR $PLURGE?

Organic bedding and clothing have gotten a lot of press lately. They are better for the environment, but you don't *need* them, and some organic fabrics, like wool, can actually irritate delicate skin. Just stick with 100 percent cotton that's soft and lightweight.

Mom Tip!

"When making up the crib, layer on two crib sheets, with a plastic mattress cover/liner in between. That way, if your baby spits up or has a leaky diaper in the night, you can just strip off the top layer without having to change the whole bed."

pink, or bright lime, neon orange, and electric blue—as are patterns: polka-dots and paisleys, ginghams and stripes. You can take your pick from princesses, fairies, hearts, and flowers to planes, trains, and automobiles.

Whatever your style, there are a few things to keep in mind when selecting bedding for your baby's crib:

Fitted sheet This is the one piece of bedding your baby will be in direct contact with much of the time, so consider what it's made of. Cotton is best, and cotton jersey is especially soft and easy to stretch over a crib mattress. Man-made fabrics, like polyester, can irritate sensitive skin (and research has shown that nonsynthetic fibers in the crib may reduce a baby's chance of developing asthma). In winter, consider cotton flannel sheets for extra warmth and coziness. You should also make sure that the sheet fits tightly around the mattress: If a corner were to pop off, it could pose a suffocation hazard.

▼ ON THE BRIGHT SIDE: IF NURSERY BEDDING (AND DÉCOR) IN PRIMARY COLORS IS YOUR PREFERENCE, CHECK OUT IKEA.

▲ CHEAP (AND CHIC!) SHEETS: AMY COE'S FRESH, COLORFUL LINE FOR TARGET IS REASONABLY PRICED ($5–$90).

23

GIZMOS & GADGETS

Changing a crib sheet can be a challenge: You practically have to lift the entire mattress out of the bed to get the sheet on. To the rescue: **The Quick Zip Crib Sheet** ($33; cloudsandstars. com), a fitted sheet with a rectangular panel that zips on and off for laundering.

Bumpers The point of these padded fabric panels that wrap around the inside of the crib (they attach to the slats, usually with fabric that can be tied in bows) is to make the crib feel cozy and also to protect an active baby from bumping up against the hard sides of the crib or getting a teeny foot or arm caught between the slats. The jury's out on whether they're necessary; some experts think they're a suffocation hazard. To be safe, don't opt for a bumper that's soft and fluffy. Tie the bumper as tightly as you can to the crib, making sure there are no gaps between it and the crib slats. Remove the bumper as soon as your baby can pull to standing (at around 9 months); she could use as a step to launch herself out of the crib.

Blankets, quilts, and duvet covers Like bumpers, these items can pose a suffocation hazard. Go ahead and purchase baby blankets (that cute quilt can double as a cheery wall hanging), but don't use them until your baby is a year old, advises the American Academy of Pediatrics. Some experts are more pragmatic, and say that a small, crib-size blanket is okay once a baby can lift her head and push the blanket off of her (around 6 months). Until then, on chilly nights, put your baby to bed in a blanket sleeper,

THE NURSERY

A number of moms in our survey swore that teddy bears that make womb noises (like a heart-beat) soothed their babies. One to try: the **Womb Sounds Mommy Bear** ($20; target.com).

fleecy footed pajamas, or some other snug-fitting nightwear. Also, avoid any blankets (or bumpers, for that matter) adorned with loose parts, like decorative buttons or appliqués that aren't sewn on tightly, that a curious baby might be able to pull off and get into her mouth.

Crib skirts We mention these because they're often sold as part of a bedding set and they can give a crib a more "finished" look. Some don't fit very well on cribs that have drawers underneath and can get in the way when you're trying to pull the drawer out. On the other hand, a crib skirt can create a perfect hiding place for storage bins and such, and they do add a more polished look to a crib.

▼ CRIB SKIRTS, LIKE THIS ONE FROM POTTERY BARN ($59), CAN EXTEND THE THEME OF YOUR NURSERY'S DÉCOR.

CHANGING TABLES

IT'S ABSOLUTELY TRUE THAT you could change your baby in her crib or on a bed or sofa (and there will be those times when it's necessary), but for the sake of your back and your sanity, having a designated area for diaper duty, where you won't have to bend over uncomfortably and where you can keep all your supplies at hand, is a plus.

When it comes to selecting a changing table, you have two basic options, with several variations of each:

A "SINGLE-PURPOSE" CHANGING TABLE In other words, a simple table with raised sides on the top and shelves underneath for storage. Styles range from ultra simple, like the solid-wood, single-shelf changing table in **IKEA's SNIGLAR series** ($29.99), to more elaborate versions with, say, a drawer and a cabinet underneath, or furniture-like styling—for instance, curved legs meant to mimic the shape of currently popular sleigh beds (and cribs) or Jenny Lind spindles.

A DRESSER/CHANGING TABLE COMBO This is usually configured as a three-drawer dresser with raised sides around the perimeter of the top. Ideally the top can be removed and the dresser used as a permanent piece of furniture. Some combination changing tables are part of bigger pieces of furniture—say, a dresser that's connected to a taller bureau or small armoire. And some dressers aren't sold as changing tables per se but can be temporarily converted with tops that are purchased separately: Changing table toppers are available for several of **Pottery Barn Kids'** basic dressers for around $150 to $200; the dressers themselves are in the $600 to $700 range. **IKEA** offers toppers at $20 each.

▶ IF YOU'RE GOING FOR A DRESSER WITH A CHANGING TABLE TOPPER, CHOOSE A CLASSIC DESIGN, LIKE THIS ONE FROM POTTERY BARN ($549), SO THE FURNITURE CAN GROW WITH YOUR CHILD.

Which you choose will boil down to budget and decorating style. If you view the changing table as a temporary item in the nursery, one that will be relegated to the attic or a yard sale as soon as your baby's no longer willing to take her diaper changes lying down (and for some kids this can happen as soon as they can walk), a simple changing table should suit you just fine. But if you're perfectly happy to spend a little more and have a piece of real furniture that you can use in your child's room for years to come, a combo unit is the way to go.

WHAT TO LOOK FOR WHEN CHOOSING EITHER TYPE OF CHANGING TABLE:

◆ **Solid, sturdy construction** Look for a table that's stable and doesn't jiggle when you gently push on it. This is especially important for single-purpose tables; combos tend to be inherently sturdy, since they're a true piece of furniture. Check underneath the top surface to make sure that it's well supported; for example, look for a slat or slats running from side to side. If you assemble the table yourself, follow directions precisely and tighten all screws completely.

◆ **Raised sides** This is optional. A changing table that doesn't have raised sides can be made safe with a separately-purchased contoured pad. (See page 29 for details about changing table accessories.)

◆ **Easily-accessed storage** This is important both for convenience and safety: You'll want to be able to easily reach a fresh diaper, the wipes box, and the rash cream without taking your eyes off your baby. Nothing beats the access provided by the open shelving of a standard changing table, but you can get as much grab-and-change convenience with a combo table that has a top with extra space for supplies. (Barring that, consider installing a shelf above the changing table.)

▲ IKEA'S BASIC CHANGING TABLE ($29.99), IS A NICE OPTION IF YOU ALREADY HAVE CLOTHING STORAGE IN A CLOSET WITH DRAWERS, OR AN ARMOIRE.

◆ **A pad** Not all changing tables are sold with pads, and even if the table you select does include one, it may not seem cushy enough for your baby's comfort. (Often, the pads that come with changing tables that have raised sides are flat and thin.) In that case, you may want to switch it out for one that's thicker and more comfortable.

◆ **A strap** for securing the baby to the table. More than 2,000 children wind up in the emergency room after tumbling off changing tables each year. The risk of falls is greatest when a baby is between 7 and 10 months old and rolling over on her own. A strap that fits across her middle will help to prevent falls, along with the raised sides of the table and/or the contoured sides of the pad. (None of these measures is foolproof, and you shouldn't let them give you a false sense of security: NEVER leave a baby unattended on a changing table, no matter how tightly she's strapped in or how young she is.) Not all changing tables have this feature, but don't let it stop you from purchasing a table that's just right in every other way. You can buy a pad with a belt.

Mom Tip!

"If your home has more than one story, set up changing stations on each floor stocked with diapers, wipes, and a change of clothes so you don't have to go up or down stairs every time you need to change the baby."

◄ THE TOPPER ON THIS LAND OF NOD CHANGING TABLE COMES OFF TO MAKE AN INSTANT "GROWN-UP" DRESSER ($119).

TURNING A DRESSER INTO A CHANGING TABLE:

Mom Tip!

"I keep a bottle of Purell on my changing table for quick post-change hand sanitizing."

If you don't have room in your nursery or budget for a changing table, you can easily convert an existing dresser or other surface, like a bathroom counter, into a temporary one simply by outfitting it with a pad. All changing table pads sold apart from changing tables are now contoured, meaning the two long sides, and sometimes the short sides, slope downwards toward the middle to create a "trough" for the baby to lie in while being changed. Make sure the pad you purchase has a safety belt and a nonslip surface and is made of vinyl-covered foam for easy cleaning. Changing table pads cost between $20 and $30.

You'll also want a changing pad cover. These are usually made of easy-to-wash terry cloth and come in a variety of colors, so you can easily find one that coordinates with the color scheme of your baby's room. Make sure the cover you buy is designed to fit the pad you have, both in terms of dimension and style (flat pad vs. contoured one). Also note that if you're using a contoured pad with a safety belt, you should pick a cover that has slits in it for the strap. Use the same rule for buying covers as you do for crib sheets: Get three, one for the changing table, one for the washer, and one freshly-laundered one to have on hand in case of accidents.

ROCKERS & GLIDERS

ROCKING CHAIRS have come a long way since Whistler's Mother posed in hers. The ones designed for the nursery are usually well-padded and fully-upholstered—and these days make up a small minority of seating designed for the nursery: Most moms-to-be opt for gliders, which move back and forth on the same plane, much like the old-fashioned gliders that graced many a front porch in your grandparents' day. (Classic wooden rocking chairs are still an option, but chances are you'll have to look beyond the baby store or nursery aisles to find one. Target does have a couple on its website.)

Many moms in our survey ranked their gliders as a favorite purchase—a nursery must-have. One reported, "My glider was a lifesaver! Nine years later, I could still spend all day in it." Another claimed her Dutailier gilder and otto-man were worth every penny.

Because *you'll* ultimately be the one sitting in it, we highly recommend you test-drive a few chairs before purchasing one, even if you plan to buy online. Stores like Babies 'R' Us and BuyBuy Baby usually have rows and rows of gliders set out for prospective parents to try.

WHAT TO LOOK (AND FEEL) FOR:

◆ **Sturdy construction** The frame should be of solid wood, and feel stable, not rickety. The parts of the chair should fit together cleanly, and any hardware, such as screws, shouldn't be exposed. Gliders have lots of moving parts; inspect them closely to make sure there are no places where curious little fingers could get pinched.

◆ **A smooth rocking or gliding action** The chair should only move forward and back; if it jiggles from side to side as well, skip it.

◆ **Good back support** So far, no one's making gliders with special lumbar support (a small pillow will take care of that, if needed), but you'll still want to make sure the chair back comes up high enough to feel comfortable.

$KIP, $AVE, OR $PLURGE?

Found the chair of your dreams, but not sure if you should spring for the matching ottoman? It may well be worth it: Elevating your legs can help take pressure off your back, especially while you're nursing, and besides, it just feels good. Most ottomans sold as accessories to specific gliders also glide, making it easy to keep that gentle movement going. Expect to pay around $200 for an ottoman.

◆ **Well-positioned arms** Make sure the arms of the chair hit at a height that's comfortable for you. Also, think in terms of where they'll be in relation to your baby's head when she's lying in your arms: You don't want the chair bumping against that delicate little soft spot.

◆ **A roomy seat** The chair should be large enough for feeding your baby. This is especially important if you plan to breastfeed, because chances are you'll use some sort of nursing pillow, many of which are c-shaped and wrap around your waist: You'll need your chair to be wide enough to accommodate the several extra inches on each side of you the pillow will require. You can also scoot to one side of the chair to make sure that there's room for a toddler or older child to snuggle in next to you.

◆ **The right height and depth** You should be able to bend your knees comfortably when your backside is against the back of the chair; likewise, your feet should be flat on the floor when your knees are bent. If you're petite, it may be hard to find a glider that fits you exactly; pillows, stools, and ottomans can help.

◆ **Comfortable padding** The amount of padding on your chair will depend on the style you choose (mostly wooden or fully upholstered; see page 32 for more), and what feels best to you is a matter of personal comfort. (So don't skip the test-driving part when you're shopping!)

◆ **Easy-to-clean upholstery** The first time your little bundle of joy burps a mouthful of formula over your shoulder and all over the back of the chair, you'll appreciate removable slipcovers that can be tossed in the washer—or at least pretreated fabric that you can wipe clean with a damp cloth. Don't opt for anything that requires more maintenance than that!

◆ **Side pockets for storage** These are optional but can come in handy for holding burp cloths, pacifiers, books, and toys for the baby, or magazines, water bottles, and the telephone for you.

◀ DOUBLE YOUR PLEASURE: BUY AN OTTOMAN THAT GLIDES ALONG WITH YOUR CHAIR, LIKE THIS SET FROM DUTAILIER (AROUND $700).

31

THE STYLES:

UPHOLSTERED ROCKERS They tend to be both beautiful—like overstuffed armchairs—and pricey. Since they're mostly sold at higher-end stores and websites, you'll pay a premium—typically upwards of $600 or so.

PLAIN WOODEN ROCKERS AND GLIDERS Not the most comfortable choice, but certainly the most economical, especially if you like a minimal look and don't mind a lack of padding. (You'll probably have a tough time finding a basic wooden rocking chair in a baby store.)

PADDED OR UPHOLSTERED GLIDERS Some gliders have padding on just the back and seat; some also have padded arms. The padding may or may not be removable; if it's not, make sure the fabric can be wiped clean. Fully-upholstered models look like easy chairs: The gliding mechanism is hidden under the fabric. Some are slip-covered, which makes them especially easy to keep clean (as long as the fabric is machine-washable).

SWIVEL GLIDERS These are relatively new: The chair not only glides back and forth, it also can twist from side to side like an office chair, making it super easy to turn and reach for something without disturbing your baby as she sleeps or nurses.

DOUBLEWIDE GLIDERS Also new-ish, these are about the size of a chair-and-a-half. They're perfect if you already have a child (and didn't buy a glider the first time around), so need to make room not just for baby, but also for her doting (or jealous!) older sibling. If you have or are expecting twins, this might be the chair for you as well.

◀ UPHOLSTERED GLIDERS, LIKE THE DREAM ROCKER AND OTTOMAN FROM POTTERY BARN KIDS ($1,148–$1,798 FOR THE SET), LOOK GREAT, BUT TAKE UP SPACE.

▲ GRACO'S IMONITOR ($85) COMES WITH TWO PARENT UNITS, SO YOU CAN LEAVE THEM IN DIFFERENT ROOMS.

Mom Tip!

"I work from home, so I chose a monitor with lights that flash when the baby cries. If I'm on the phone while my baby's sleeping, I turn down the volume on the monitor and rely on the lights to tell me when naptime's over—rather than have a business call interrupted by her wails."

IF YOU LIVE IN A SMALL HOUSE or apartment, you may not even need a monitor. But if you're going to be outside of hearing distance of your baby when she's sleeping in her crib or hanging around in her play yard, you'll want to be able to keep tabs on her. Monitors come in two varieties: audio and video.

Here's what you need to know about each:

AUDIO MONITORS These let you listen in on your baby's every coo and cry. Most consist of a transmitter that you plug into an outlet in the room where your baby is and a receiver that stays with you. Both transmitters and receivers may also have rechargeable batteries, so you won't always be limited to areas with an electrical outlet when using either; and many are the size of, say, a wallet or iPod, and portable, thanks to a wrist strap or fanny-pack-like attachment. You can also buy a monitor with more than one receiver, meaning both parents can listen in on the baby from different parts of the house.

Some monitors come with an intercom feature, so that you can talk to your baby from another room—a nice perk if she's easily calmed by your voice. Still others allow you to play music for your baby.

The most important thing to keep in mind when buying an audio baby monitor is the frequency: If it's the same or close to that of your cordless phone (most newer ones are 2.4 gigahertz or 900 megahertz), you're guaranteed to get static or "cross talk." Expect to spend about $20 to $90 for an audio monitor. One we like: **Graco's Décor monitor** ($40; gracobaby.com), which comes in a variety of pastel hues to coordinate with the nursery. Several moms in our survey recommend the **Angelcare Movement Sensor** (about $90).

▶ ALL-IN-ONE: THE MOTOROLA C51 IS A CORDLESS PHONE, ANSWERING MACHINE, AND VIDEO BABY MONITOR (ABOUT $100 FOR THE BASE).

VIDEO MONITORS Don't trust your ears? Or just can't take your eyes off your beautiful babe? Either way, you can opt for a monitor with a wall- or table-mounted camera that will send images of her to a teeny TV-like monitor (at least one company, Summer, makes one with a handheld video monitor). These are considerably more expensive than their audio counterparts (they start at about $130), but for some parents this may well be worth the peace of mind.

33

CLOTHING

IF YOU LOVED DRESSING UP DOLLS when you were a child, you're going to adore shopping for clothes for your very own, real-life baby. With designers ranging from Ralph Lauren and Dolce & Gabbana to Old Navy and Target turning out miniature lines, there's no end to the ways you can dress up your little one. And while style-wise just about anything goes, keep these guidelines in mind when putting together a mini wardrobe:

Comfort trumps cute Baby skin is as delicate as it looks and should be treated that way. Choose items made from soft, 100 percent natural fibers, especially cotton. Some synthetics can be scratchy and generally don't "breathe," allowing moisture to get trapped and irritate skin. (One exception: acrylic fleece is soft and can keep your baby warm and cozy in cold weather, and is an especially good choice for outerwear.) Wool can also rub baby skin the wrong way, so opt for the softest knits (and just in case, layer wool sweaters over a cotton tee or turtleneck). Skip stiff lace and other embellishments, which can be irritating as well.

Safety first Check that buttons are sewn on tightly and be on the lookout for any decorations that could come loose and make their way into your baby's mouth. Avoid drawstrings, which can get wrapped around a baby's neck.

Make it easy on yourself Certain features, like rows of tiny buttons, can be adorable to look at but a pain to deal with.

BABY'S FIRST WARDROBE

Technically, a layette is everything a baby needs, from T-shirts to a car seat, but for most people it simply means clothing. But which items of clothing? And how many of each?

For the first few weeks, your baby won't need a particularly varied wardrobe to stay warm and comfortable. Here are the essentials for newborns. Tear out this page (or photocopy it, or download it at parenting.com) and have it on hand when you're shopping.

HOW MANY	WHAT	WHY
1	"take-me-home" outfit	for photo ops
8	T-shirts	Newborns need an extra layer for warmth. Buy kimono shirts to start; in 8 weeks or so, you'll be ready for onesies.
3	top-and-bottom sets	for outings
4	coveralls (one-piece footed outfits, also known as "stretchies" or "sleepers")	to keep your baby comfy day and night
6	pairs of socks	to keep baby toes toasty
2	large towels (can be hooded)	to keep the chill off after baths
8	nightgowns	for comfy naps and easy-change nights
1	sweater	Babies often need an extra layer of clothing, even indoors.
2	sleep sacks	for chilly nights, in place of a blanket
12	burp cloths	to soak up you-know-what after feedings
4	receiving blankets	for swaddling and layering
2	close-fitting knit hats	Babies' heads get chilled easily.
1	brimmed hat	for sunny days
1	jacket or snowsuit	for outings in inclement weather

37

A note about sizing: Ever heard the phrase, "They grow up so fast"? Well, that applies from day one: What fits when your baby comes home from the hospital won't fit in four weeks, let alone twelve. In the beginning your infant will mostly wear T-shirts, footed coveralls, and nightgowns, so buy those in 3-month sizes. When it comes time for your baby to wear "real" outfits, purchase 6-month sizes and roll up the sleeves and pant cuffs.

LOOK FOR:
- soft, comfortable fabrics, especially cotton
- elastic-waist bottoms
- tops that slip easily over your child's head (stretchy necks and snaps or buttons at the shoulder work well)
- outfits that don't have buttons down the back (They're hard to put on and uncomfortable for your baby, who'll spend most of his time lying on his back.)

BEST PICKS

A take-me-home outfit Because the camera will be flashing when your newborn leaves the hospital, you might want his coming-out outfit to be special. Just make sure that it's easy to put on and weather-appropriate. No matter what time of year, he should be wearing a hat and his feet should be covered with socks or booties.

T-shirts The best "starter" tees for a newborn are kimono-style tops that snap at the side. They won't rub against his umbilical stump, which needs room and air to heal properly, and they're the easiest to put on. Once he's a few months old and wriggling around, the undershirts with snaps at the bottom will stay put better, and because they'll fit closely against his skin, they'll keep him warm.

Shirt and pants sets These are probably what you'll put on your baby for the occasional outing, if you feel like a footed stretchie isn't enough.

Coveralls Also called sleepers or stretchies, these one-piece outfits can be footed or not. Some moms prefer nonfooted styles, because they'll fit longer. On the other hand, footed clothing eliminates the need to pull tiny socks over tiny feet, where they may not stay. Consider how the outfit closes: One that buttons all the way up can be a pain. Snaps are much easier; just make sure they go far enough down to make it easy to slip your baby in and out of a coverall. (Most snap from neck to the ankle of one leg.) And zippers are quickest and easiest of all. **Hanna Andersson** (hannaandersson.com) has a cute line of 100 percent cotton "Zippers" (zip-up rompers).

Socks Cotton ones with a little bit of stretch are best, since you'll need to do all the work of fitting them over your infant's feet. (He won't flex his toes to make it easier!) Avoid patterned socks that might have loose strings inside that could get tangled around tiny toes.

Towels The hooded ones are cute and practical. Go for soft absorbent cotton terry cloth.

Nightgowns Buy the kind with a gathered bottom. During middle-of-the-night diaper duty, all you have to do is slip the bottom up for a quick change.

Sweater A lightweight cotton cardigan will be all your baby needs when you take him out on a warm day and will come in handy if it's chilly inside the house. Don't go for a bulky style, which makes it hard for him to wave his arms around (and which won't layer comfortably).

Sleep sacks On chilly nights, you'll bundle your baby in one of these to sleep, rather than pile on blankets. (Loose bedding, along with stuffed toys and pillows, is a suffocation hazard in a crib.) Typically made of cozy, polyester fleece, these look like what they sound like: wearable blankets, closed at the bottom and roomy enough to fit over a nightgown or stretchy. For easy diaper changes, look for a sack with an inverted zipper (meaning it zips from the bottom up). Also (and this holds true for any sleepwear), make sure it's labeled "flame-resistant."

Burp cloths Here's an area where you probably want to choose cost over cute: Cloth diapers are the best deal around. You can buy a dozen for around 10 bucks and use any that make it through your baby's first year as dust cloths.

Receiving blankets These smallish blankets are what you'll use in the first few weeks for swaddling—wrapping your little bundle up tight like a burrito. Swaddling helps newborns, who are used to the confines of the womb, feel safe and comfortable in the great, big, sprawling world. The best fabric for swaddling is plain old flannel; the fibers "adhere" to one another so that the edges of the blanket stay together.

CLOTHING

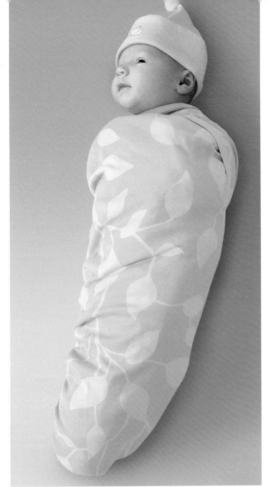

For no-brainer swaddling, try the **Miracle Blanket** ($30; miracleblanket. com), which has little pouches to tuck your baby's arms and legs into before you wrap her up. Moms also love the **SwaddleMe** blanket made by **Kiddopotamus** (left). "They're amazing!" said one mom from our survey: "They have Velcro tabs to keep the baby tightly swaddled."

HOW TO SWADDLE

Mom Tip!

"I can't say enough about swaddling your infant until she won't fit in the blanket anymore. For naps, bedtime, and soothing, swaddling was my savior."

1. On a bed or other flat surface, spread a receiving blanket out in a diamond shape (corners pointing up, down, right, and left). Fold the top corner down 5 inches or so.

2. Lay your baby on the blanket so that his head is just above the folded-down edge.

3. Holding his arms by his side, fold the right-hand corner of the blanket across his body, tucking it snugly around his arm on his left side.

4. Fold the bottom corner up.

5. Fold the left-hand corner across his body and wrap it snugly around him.

39

BEYOND THE LAYETTE

ONCE YOU'VE GOT THE NEWBORN PERIOD COVERED, you'll need clothing that fits your baby's needs as he reaches certain physical milestones. What to consider when shopping for a growing baby, stage by stage:

THE ROLLING-OVER STAGE

At around 2 to 3 months, once a baby can flip over (and in the months to come, as he reaches other physical milestones, like grabbing at toys), you'll want to dress him in clothing that stays put and won't get in his way:

◆ **T-shirts that snap at the crotch** won't ride up and bunch. Look for ones that have snaps or buttons at the necks, or an overlapping boatneck design that makes it easy to slip over that still fragile head. Rompers and bottoms that snap between the legs will save lots of time at diaper changes.

◆ **Items with smooth inner seams** that won't rub against your baby's skin. Also be on the lookout for appliqués that are attached on the inside and could be itchy.

◆ **Soft knit fabrics** Stiffer ones will be hard for your baby to test out all his new moves in.

▶ LAYER, LAYER:
YOU CAN SLIP OFF
ONE TOP IF HE
GETS TOO HOT.

▲ OVERALLS CAN BE A YEAR-ROUND WARDROBE STAPLE; JUST CHANGE WHAT'S UNDERNEATH!

THE CRAWLING STAGE

Getting around on hands and knees, something your baby will start to do between 7 and 11 months, presents a new set of needs in the baby-clothing department. Dress your little go-getter in:

◆ **Overalls.** Moms of girls, this means you especially: Dresses just won't hack it during this stage, at least not for everyday play. The nice thing about overalls is that they usually have adjustable straps, so your child can wear them into toddlerhood.

◆ **Pants that aren't too baggy.** Loose-fitting bottoms can bunch up at the knee and make it tough for your baby to move around. Elasticized cuffs at the leg (like those on sweats) help keep pant legs from riding up as well.

THE CRUISING STAGE AND BEYOND

When your baby can pull himself up to standing—anytime between 6 and 11 months—and especially when he can get around while holding onto furniture, you'll need to dress him to prevent slips. Put away any outfits with fabric feet, and let him go barefoot. If it's chilly, opt for:

◆ **Socks with rubber treads on the bottom.**

◆ **Non-skid booties.** Textured suede is good for preventing slipping. (See pages 44–45 for our favorite brands.)

GIZMOS & GADGETS

You can get a lot more wear out of crotch snap tees and other tops with garment extenders—funny-looking squares of fabric that snap onto the existing snaps of the T-shirt to literally make it longer. One brand to look for: **Garment Extenders** by **Basic Comfort,** (call 800-456-8687 for stores), $4 for three or $6 for six.

$KIP, $AVE, OR $PLURGE?

With the exception of shoes, there's nothing wrong with (and a lot to be said for!) accepting hand-me-downs; or buying preworn baby clothes. Just inspect each item carefully for stains (for aesthetic reasons) and make sure buttons are sewn on tightly, zippers are working smoothly, and snaps aren't so worn that they don't stay closed. Otherwise, approach used baby clothes in the same way that you would new ones: Go for soft and simple. You can save a lot with big-ticket items like snowsuits, that generally only see one season of wear before they're outgrown, and often end up in close-to-pristine condition.

BIBS! BIBS! BIBS!

GIZMOS & GADGETS

When dining out with a toddler, you don't always want to deal with a regular bib: A ketchup-smeared bib is a pretty gross thing to bring home along with the doggy bag. A neater alternative: disposable bibs. These are typically made of paper with a thin plastic backing, and most have a fold at the bottom to catch crumbs. Two to try: **Toss-Away Bibs by Classy Kid** ($3.99 for 20) and **Pocket Bibsters by Pampers** ($3.99 for 16).

NOTHING SAYS, "Hey, I'm a baby!" like a piece of cloth tied around the neck. Some parents with especially drooly babies like to keep their kids bibbed almost all the time, to protect both their clothes and their skin: A chin, neck, or even chest that's constantly awash in saliva can become raw and chapped very quickly. Other moms only use bibs during meals. Either way, here are your options:

NEWBORNS

Even at this stage, a bib can come in handy during feedings—like a wearable burp cloth to help catch spit-up. Choose a bib in a soft, absorbent material, like cotton terry cloth, so whatever comes out of your baby's mouth gets soaked up right away, and opt for one that has snaps or Velcro. Bibs for infants are often sold in multi-packs of ten or twelve at baby stores and general retail stores

Mom Tip!

"If you're in a pinch, you can always tuck a burp cloth into your baby's collar, or tie a restaurant's linen napkin loosely around her neck."

like K-Mart and Target (skip the fancy ones sold at boutiques), so you can keep several clean ones on hand—in the nursery, kitchen, diaper bag, etc.—while the rest are in the laundry.

OLDER BABIES

At around 6 months, your child will begin to sit up independently and start eating solid foods. Bib-wise, it's time to bring in the big guns. Look for:

◆ **A bib that protects** as much of your baby's front as possible, without getting in his way or being uncomfortable. This could be anything from a bib that's simply oversized to one that covers his chest and shoulders. Many, like the **I Play Sesame Street Best Bib Coverall,** also feature a pocket at the bottom to catch crumbs ($14.99 for a pack of three). For even more coverage, consider a smock-like bib such as the **Get Messy Bib by Babylicious,** which comes in bright, mod designs and has long sleeves, a bottom pocket, and can be wiped clean ($14; babylicious.com for stores).

◆ **A wipeable surface.** Since your baby's diet is about to become considerably more colorful (think bright peagreens and sweet potato-oranges), a bib that soaks up those colors will be more trouble than it's worth. Laminated bibs can be wiped clean with a swipe of a damp paper towel. The ones by **Icky Baby** have attractive vintage patterns on the front, terry cloth backing, and close with Velcro at one shoulder ($15; ickybaby.com for stores). Just as cute, but less pricey: **Sassy's Easy Clean Bibs with Soft Backs.** The pockets on these brightly colored laminated bibs unfold for easy cleaning, and they're easy on the wallet: $4.99 for three.

GIZMOS & GADGETS

Bib Clips are great for eating on the go. They're a set of two plastic clips that you can attach to anything from a cloth napkin to a burp cloth to create a bib ($12; babystyle.com).

▶ VELCRO CLOSURES, LIKE ON THIS BIB FROM BABYLICIOUS (ABOUT $10), ARE A NICE OPTION FOR DINERS UNDER 6 MONTHS OLD.

SHOES

WHAT YOUR BABY WEARS—or doesn't wear—on his feet depends on his age and stage of development. Here's what you need to know, from booties and beyond:

NEWBORNS

Teeny-tiny Mary Janes, wee cowboy boots, and bitsy track shoes are adorable sitting on a store shelf—but they should stay there. Infants don't need shoes, period. Confining a growing foot inside a stiff shoe will interfere with proper growth and development. When he isn't dressed in a footed outfit, however, you will want to keep your baby's feet covered and warm in chilly weather or air-conditioning. Here are some options for doing that:

SOCKS Cotton with a little stretch is easiest to slip over tiny toes. And socks with a roll-over cuff tend to stay on kicking feet best.

BOOTIES Make sure openings are wide enough to wrangle a baby's foot through, but not so wide that the foot will slide right back out. Better yet, look for styles that have some sort of feature for making it easy to slip the shoe on and then securing it around the foot, like a toggle that can be loosened and tightened, a hook-and-toggle at the heel, or a Velcro flap across the top.

▼ ELASTICIZED ANKLES, LIKE THE ONES IN ROBEEZ, ($26) ARE KEY FOR KEEPING BOOTIES ON TINY FEET.

Some baby shoe brands we love (some will take your child into the toddler stage):

Robeez A must-have for many moms, this popular brand of shoe is both cute and remarkably clever. The "uppers" are of super-supple leather, the soles of textured, nonskid suede, and they come in dozens of cute designs. The brilliance of Robeez is the soft band of elastic that fits around the ankle to make it easy to slip the shoes on and almost impossible for them to slip off. Robeez also makes ankle-high booties with a fleece lining ($26 for shoes, $37 for booties; robeez.com and at baby boutiques). You can also find less expensive knockoffs (like Target's Circo brand, $12.99).

44

Isabooties Similar to Robeez, with non-skid soles and soft elastic around the ankle, these baby shoes are adorned with a pretty band of ribbon ($26; isabooties.com).

Face shoes by Vincent Talk about happy feet! These comfy slip-ons, available in six colors, feature a smiling face, a wide opening, and snug Velcro closures ($25; vincentshoestore.com).

▲ ISABOOTIES ($26) CAN BE MACHINE -WASHED AND -DRIED.

Gucio With wide soles for balance and extra-flexible toes, these funky handmade shoes are perfect for a toddler's uneven steps. Sizes 8 and up also have a double-thick sole for playground pounding ($48; toddlertreads.com).

▲ FACE SHOES BY VINCENT ($25) ALSO HAVE NONSKID RUBBER SOLES.

▲ THE THIN FLEXIBLE SOLES OF GUCIO TODDLER SHOES ($48) MAKE FOR EASY TODDLER WALKING.

OLDER BABIES

Around 5 months, when your baby discovers his feet, you might switch from plain socks to:

◆ Brightly colored socks that take advantage of his growing interest in the world around him: He'll love watching his toes wiggling in a pair of lime green socks. (Give him plenty of sockless time as well: Babies love to play with their toes and even suck on them.)

◆ Socks and booties with little attached toys or rattles are meant to be used as entertainment rather than real clothing, but they really can hold a baby's interest. Keep his favorite pair in the car or stroller and whip them out when he gets antsy on a long ride. Just make sure that anything adorning a pair of socks or booties is securely attached.

CRUISING BABIES AND TODDLERS

Once your baby starts getting around on his own two feet, whether he's hanging on to a coffee table, holding your hands, or taking his first solo steps, he's ready for real shoes, right? Yes—and no. Inside the house, unless your home is really chilly, bare is best for little feet just learning to walk. Without shoes in the way, tiny toes can flex and grip the floor, which helps both with balance and with strengthening foot muscles. Outside, or on cold, uncarpeted floors, teeny feet need some protection.

45

10 STEPS TO BUYING YOUR TODDLER'S FIRST PAIR OF SHOES

1. Make sure they fit. Don't try to order your baby's first shoes online. Go to a children's shoe store and have a salesperson measure both feet: Most babies' tootsies vary by as much as a half size.

2. Do the thumb test. Your toddler's longest toe should be a thumb's width (about half an inch) from the tip of the shoe.

3. Hone in on the heel. If it looks loose or slips up and down as your toddler walks, the friction could cause blisters. If the heel looks tight, it will be equally uncomfortable.

4. Sort out the shape. The dimensions of a child's shoe should approximate the shape of his foot, so choose squares or ovals.

5. Get comfortable. Kids' footwear should be porous and flexible; you should be able to bend a child's shoe in your hand without much effort.

Cloth, canvas, and leather all stretch, bend, and "breathe," while rubber and plastic are stiff and cause feet to sweat excessively.

6. Check the tread. Moderately grooved soles will help a wobbly toddler stay upright. Don't go for treads that are too deep, though, or shoe bottoms that are slick and slippery.

7. Keep his socks on. Make sure your child has on the kind of socks he'll be wearing with the shoes he's trying on.

8. Watch your child's reaction. If he seems uncomfortable or has trouble walking in a particular shoe, no matter how cute, skip it.

9. Don't buy big. It's true that toddlers outgrow their shoes every three months or so, but if you're tempted to try to get a few extra months out of your purchase, forget it: Too-big shoes are tough to walk in and could even be unsafe.

10. Steer clear of trends. Pointy boots, clogs, and other high-fashion footwear won't provide the support and stability a novice walker needs.

◀ VELCRO CLOSURES ON SHOES, LIKE THESE BY STRIDE RITE ($30), TAKE THE FUSS OUT OF FOOTWEAR.

Children's shoe retailers, like **stride rite,** can usually direct you to the best styles and brands for your child. (Some kids have particularly wide or fat or narrow feet, so certain shoes will fit better than others.) You'll often get the same service at a **department store** or a **specialty shoe store** for kids, though these stores will mostly carry expensive, high-end, often European (and admittedly beautiful) shoes. Keep in mind that your child will outgrow those $50 Elefantens before they're barely worn.

One of the best places to purchase little kid shoes is **Payless.** If you're confident about fitting your toddler's foot correctly, check out the variety of styles offered at this inexpensive chain store, or buy "extra" shoes there once you've had your child properly fitted. You'll find everything from classic high-top leather baby shoes to light-up sneakers and ones featuring characters like Dora and Thomas—the types of shoes that your older toddler might actually want to keep on his feet. Best of all, Payless designers incorporate baby shoe essentials such as flexible soles, nonskid treads, optional wide widths in select styles (to accommodate baby fat), and easy-on, easy-off features (for example, Velcro closures under faux buckles). You'll find similar offerings at Target.

▲ DORA SLIDES ($14.99) CAN SATISFY YOUR CHILD'S DESIRE FOR CHARACTER CLOTHING FOR NOT TOO MUCH MONEY.

A note about hand-me-downs: Most toddlers outgrow their shoes after three months or so, often leaving behind footwear that looks barely used. Is it okay to save those shoes for a younger sibling (or buy used shoes from a consignment store, or for that matter, use the ones your sister-in-law packed in with the last batch of hand-me-downs from your niece)? Some experts say no, claiming that once a shoe conforms to one child's foot, it'll interfere with proper foot development if worn by a different child. Others take a more pragmatic approach and say that if you know that a pair of hand-me-down shoes were worn only sporadically, and if the heels aren't worn down and other parts of the shoe haven't become misshapen, it's probably okay for a child who's been walking for some time to wear them. (Don't put preworn shoes on a brand-new toddler.)

▲ THE GRIPPY SOLE ON THESE STRIDE RITE SNEAKERS ($30) HELPS NEW WALKERS STAY ON THEIR FEET.

47

OUTERWEAR

IN COOL WEATHER, there's no need to overbundle your baby: He'll need just one layer more than you're wearing (a light jacket over a sweater over a cotton top to your jacket over a shirt, for example). But when the weather outside is frightful, you'll want to keep him toasty. What you'll need to make sure your baby stays warm and dry in winter or cold climates:

JACKETS Newborns and babies too young to walk or play outside really don't need a one-piece snowsuit: Their exposure to the elements will be limited to the amount of time it takes to get them from the house to the car, from the car to the supermarket, and back. In strollers, a blanket or stroller bag will keep their legs warm. Features to look for in a jacket:

◆ **Warmth** Choose a jacket made of a warm material, like polyester fleece. Down is good if the outer material if waterproof. Avoid cotton; if it gets wet, it stays wet.

◆ **Built-in mittens** This doesn't matter so much for a newborn, but once your baby discovers his hands, you'll have a tough time keeping mittens on them. Built-in mittens are just flaps of fabric attached to the sleeve that fold over a baby's hands.

◆ **An elasticized hood** This is a safety precaution: Draw-strings can get wrapped around necks and present a choking hazard.

SNOWSUITS These are a more expensive option than a jacket, so if you decide to invest in one for a young infant, or if you're shopping for a baby who's walking and who's likely to play outside—especially in the snow—you'll want to spend wisely. Look for:

◆ **A wind- and water-resistant fabric.** Down or a polyester fleece such as Polartec are ideal chill-chasers. Make sure the outside of a down-filled snowsuit is water-resistant; a nylon shell is a good option. Both **L.L. Bean** (llbean.com) and **Lands' End** (landsend.com, and at Sears stores), famous for adult and big kid outerwear, sell excellent snowsuits for babies made of the same materials as their larger outerwear. Prices range from around $30 for a simple polyester fleece suit at L.L. Bean to almost $60 for a 650-fill goose down snowsuit with a quilted polyester shell at Lands' End.

▼ ONCE YOUR CHILD IS OLD ENOUGH TO TRUDGE THROUGH THE SNOW—ABOUT 2 YEARS—YOU'LL APPRECIATE A WATERPROOF SNOWSUIT LIKE THIS ONE FROM LANDS' END ($59.50).

48

◆ **A zipper that runs ankle to knee.** It's tough enough to stuff a baby into a snowsuit without having to cram his legs into a small opening.

◆ **Built-in mittens for young babies.** Some snowsuits also have roll-over cuffs on the legs to help keep little feet warm.

◆ **Cuffs that fit tightly at ankle and wrist.** These will keep the cold from seeping into the sleeves and pant legs of snow suits worn by older babies and toddlers, who'll be wearing separate mittens and boots or shoes. Look for elastic at the cuffs, or better yet, Velcro tabs that let you adjust the tightness of the cuffs.

MITTENS Gloves are too hard to maneuver over a baby's fingers, and besides, mittens are warmer because they keep fingers close together. To make it super easy, opt for thumb-less mitts. One irresistibly cute option: **BearHands** mittens, which resemble a furry little paw and will keep little fingers toasty warm ($12 and up; bearhands.net).

◀ MITTENS ON A STRING, LIKE THESE FROM KINDERCASH-MERE, ($45) CAN BE A BIG TIME- (AND MONEY-) SAVER!

HATS On a merely chilly (rather than downright cold) day, a hat or cap may be a more comfortable and practical way to keep your baby's head warm than the hood on his jacket or snowsuit. On a frigid day, a tight-fitting cap can also add an extra layer of warmth under a hood. Either way, buy a hat that covers your baby's entire head—a baseball style cap won't be warm enough—and preferably one with ear flaps. Wool or cotton knits are fine on dry days, but in any type of precipitation, opt for a head covering that's water-resistant. A cap that fastens under the chin is more likely to stay on. Also, make sure any hat or cap you put on your baby doesn't tend to slip down over his eyes.

▼ MAKE SURE THE LINING OF ANY HAT IS SUPER-SOFT.

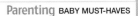

49

◄ A GOOD TREAD ON SNOW BOOTS (LIKE THESE LANDS' END SNOW FLURRIES; $25) HELPS A NEW WALKER GET STEADIER FOOTING ON THE SLIPPERY STUFF.

SKIP THE SCARF

Scarves can wrap around a child's neck and strangle him, and can also be a suffocation hazard. Layer a turtleneck under your baby's outerwear to keep his neck warm.

BOOTS Infants and prewalkers don't need boots, but a toddler who's walking well might. The key feature to look for when buying snow boots for a very young child is some sort of opening to make it easy to slip them on and off: Imagine trying to stuff a squirmy child's foot through the narrow top of a boot! A few options that fit the easy-on/easy-off bill:

Lands' End Snow Flurry Boots They're designed to open extra wide, and close with Velcro (no zipper to get caught in the fabric of a snowsuit or pants leg). They're also insulated with Thermolite and have a moisture-wicking lining; so feet stay dry even if snow gets inside ($25; landsend.com).

Moppet boots by Kamik A big, self-gripping strap earns these weatherproof boots points for being easy to get on and off fast ($35; kamik.com).

Snow Tread boots by L.L. Bean The rubber sole guarantees these'll last through more than one little snow bunny ($30; llbean.com).

Cold Front boots by stride rite The side strap makes it easy to get these boots nice and snug—to keep out snow as well as fit easily under pants ($32; striderite.com).

SUNWEAR

GIZMOS & GADGETS

Washing your child's clothing in **Rit Sun Guard,** a laundry additive, will substantially increase its SPF; the treated clothing will stay UV-protective for about 20 washings ($2 per box; www.sunguard-sunprotection.com and grocery stores).

THE GREATEST RISKS TO A BABY IN SUMMER or hot climates are overheating and sun exposure. A single blistering sunburn in childhood doubles the risk of melanoma in later life, so the American Academy of Pediatrics recommends that babies under 6 months be kept out of direct sunlight altogether and that older babies stay out of the sun between 10 A.M. and 4 P.M., when the rays are most intense. But given that it's tough to avoid the sun completely, you'll need to dress your baby so that he's as protected as possible when the two of you are out, whether you're going to the supermarket for an hour or the beach for the day. Here's a guide to dressing your baby for hot weather:

HATS Whether your baby is bald as a bowling ball or sporting a full head of curls, his tender scalp is as susceptible to sunburn as the rest of him. Look for a hat that will shade not just the front of his face, like a baseball cap, but also his ears (because they stick out, they're especially prone to burning, as is his nose) and the back of his neck. A classic sun hat with a wide brim that goes all the way around does the trick. A snap or Velcro closure might seem quickest and easiest to deal with, but these can't always be adjusted to be snug enough and are easily unfastened by tiny fingers. Look for one that ties under the chin so that it's more likely to stay on—make it just tight enough and you can double-knot the bow so that it won't come undone. Another option: styles with a flap of fabric that runs around the back from ear to ear, as well as a wide visor at the front. You can find the original brand of this type of hat, **Flap Happy,** at many kids' clothing stores (go to flaphappy.com for specific retailers), but there are plenty of knockoffs. Sun hats for babies come in a variety of fabrics, from 100 percent cotton to nylon; cotton will be coolest, but for adequate sun protection it should be tightly-woven.

▲ FLAP HAPPY SUN HATS (ABOUT $12) PROTECT DELICATE SKIN ON THE BACK OF THE NECK AS WELL AS YOUR BABY'S FACE.

TOPS, BOTTOMS, AND ONE-PIECE OUTFITS Dress your newborn or very young baby (under 6 months) in long sleeves and full-length bottoms made from lightweight cotton with a tight weave; loosely knit fabrics allow more

51

sun rays through. (Sunscreen is not recommended for full-body use on babies under 6 months, but it's fine to use a broad-spectrum sunscreen with an SPF of at least 15 on areas not covered by clothing.)

Just be careful not to overbundle your infant. The same rule applies in hot weather as in cool: Put just one more layer of clothing on your baby than you're wearing.

A baby over 6 months can wear shorts and short sleeve tops, sleeveless dresses, and the like, but will need to be sunscreened fully. Again, lightweight cotton is the best fabric for summer: It "breathes," which keeps your child cool, and allows sweat to evaporate rather than stick to skin and cause irritation.

▲ BUDDING BATHING BEAUTIES: CHECK OUT OLD NAVY'S CUTE ONE-PIECES, BIKINIS, AND TANKINIS ($14.50).

SOCKS, SHOES, AND SANDALS If your baby's outfit isn't footed, just slip a pair of thin cotton socks over his feet to protect them. If he's in a stroller, remember that the bottoms of his feet are exposed if not covered.

Beginner walkers should wear shoes, which typically provide more support than sandals. Canvas sneakers with a flexible sole (over cotton socks) are your best bet in summer; they're cooler than leather. And they can be tossed in the wash after an especially grimy play day. Toddlers who've been walking for a while and have got their bearings can wear sandals. The best for kids this age have a semi-closed front to protect little toes and a closed back for heel and ankle support. A leather sandal will hold up best (the spaces between the straps let air flow through), and one that buckles rather than Velcros will be more likely to stay on. You'll find kids' sandals that meet these criteria wherever good-quality children's shoes are sold—from stride rite and department stores to Target and Payless.

◀ OLD NAVY SELLS BOYS' SWIMWEAR AS SEPARATES, SO YOU CAN MIX AND MATCH AS YOU PLEASE (ABOUT $10 PER PIECE).

Mom Tip!

"I cut the mesh liner out of my toddler's swim trunks. This way, sand from the beach doesn't get trapped inside— less itchy for him, less messy for me."

SWIMSUITS What's cuter than a really itsy-bitsy teeny-weeny yellow polka-dot bikini? Or a tiny pair of surfer trunks, complete with a palm tree motif? You can find both, and more, among the choices in min swimwear. Whether your baby *needs* a swimsuit is a different question. Some experts feel that kids under 6 months should be kept out of the water, because they aren't able to regulate their body temperature and could get too cold, even on a very hot day or in a heated pool. If you're bringing your infant along to the beach or neighborhood pool, he doesn't really need to dress for the occasion;

long sleeves and full-length bottoms in breathable cotton will keep him cool and protected from the sun.

An older baby or toddler can go in the pool (or ocean or lake), in which case a swimsuit is a good idea. For the bottom, a swim diaper will suffice, but he really should have some sort of top on to give added protection from the sun (though you should use sunblock underneath). A cotton T-shirt would do, but won't dry out as quickly as a top made from Lycra, nylon, or other classic swimsuit material. Consider both a top and bottom for swimming that covers as much territory as possible. You can also try miniature "rash" shirts for babies—the body-hugging, short-sleeved tops worn by surfers. Pair one with your little boy's trunks, or sub one for the top to your daughter's two-piece suit. If you'd prefer a more classic style on your little girl, a tankini is a good choice: The top will cover her belly, and the separate bottom will make diaper changes easier.

▲ BABY BANZ SUNGLASSES ($15) WERE DEVELOPED BY A DAD IN AUSTRALIA, WHERE THEY KNOW THEIR SUN PROTECTION!

SUNGLASSES are a good way to protect a baby's eyes and make it easier to see in bright sunshine. The trick is keeping them on: Look for shades that have a strap that Velcros in the back, rather than traditional arms that wrap around the ears. The glasses will be less likely to slip off, and since they're more comfortable, your baby will be less likely to pull them off. Some to try: **Baby Banz,** which have an adjustable neoprene strap and offer 100 percent UVA protection ($15; babybanz.com); and **Julbo Looping Sunglasses,** which are symmetrical, meaning there's no upside down, and sport soft rubber on the bridge and temples for no-slip comfort ($25; julboinc.com).

GIZMOS & GADGETS

Clothing with built-in sun protection (called UPF) is becoming increasingly popular. A UPF rating of 50 means that a fabric will allow only 1/50th of the sun's UV rays to pass through. Only clothes with a UPF of 15 to 50 may be labeled as sun-protective. But are they necessary? Certainly not for everyday, especially if you have a newborn, whom you'll be keeping well covered and in the shade. But if you're planning to spend a lot of time in the sun with your child, and/or if he is fair-skinned, you might consider UPF swimwear. The Skin Care Foundation recommends the one-piece rompers sold by **Coolibar** (coolibar.com). These long-sleeved, to-the-ankle rompers are made of SUNTECT, a lightweight fabric that blocks 98 percent of UV rays. They come in pink and blue, feature a snap-close bottom for easy diaper access, and cost about $30.

53

SOME FAVORITE BRANDS

BABY CLOTHES ARE BIG BUSINESS, and it would be impossible to mention every company that makes them. Our criteria for the top picks here?

◆ **Affordable price points** After all, you're lucky to get three months out of newborn clothing, and a season out of bigger kids' clothing, so why spend a premium?

◆ **Durability** These brands will stand up to multiple washings, as well as wear-and-tear.

◆ **Comfort** Soft fabrics, well-finished seams, and non-scratchy appliqués are all musts.

◆ **Safety** This applies particularly to baby clothes.

◆ **Style** Fashion-wise, we've come a long way, baby: these stores offer duds that are cute without being cutesy, colorful without being garish.

Carter's and **Gerber** (creator of the Onesie snap-crotch tee) make reliable, affordable wardrobe staples like nightgowns, undershirts, and one-piece footed sleepers and rompers. Styles and colors are classic baby—sweet pastels, bright primaries, cute animals, etc. And you can often buy coordinating extras, like receiving blankets and rattles (carters.com and gerber.com).

The Gap and **Old Navy** Tiny trendsetters get their goods from these two major ubiquitous clothing stores. Besides making mini-versions of many of the same styles the companies sell for grown-ups (check out the Gap's super-soft, flannel-lined blue jeans for babies, which feature an elasticized waist and snaps for easy diaper changes), both retailers offer adorable 100 percent cotton pj's, one-piece rompers, coordinating separates, socks, and even shoes. There's almost always a sale rack loaded with still-in-season bargains in stores, so try to hold off on buying anything at full price; chances are next week it'll be marked down. The Gap is a little pricier than Old Navy, but the difference in quality is usually negligible (gap.com and oldnavy.com).

Gymboree Gymboree sells only clothing for kids, from newborn to size 12. The store usually features several different "collections" per season, with a variety of items in each. (For example, there might be a line of safari-themed clothing for little boys, with shirts featuring lions, overalls with a tiger-patch on the front, caps with the same tiger or lion above the visor, and so forth; everything can be mixed and matched.) Most

Mom Tip!

"If you like Gap or Old Navy and live near one, you can save a lot of money by getting a Gap or Old Navy credit card (either can be used for savings at both stores). For every $200 you spend, you'll get a $10 coupon with your bill; plus, you'll get 10 percent off any purchases made on the first Tuesday of each month, both in stores and online. They're constantly sending coupons—it's a great deal if you pay your bills in full and on time."

items are of high-quality fabrics (100 percent cottons and nice fleeces), and are well made and affordable. Gymboree also sells accessories like tights and leggings, baby blankets, and toys. You can buy online, or at one of the chain's many stores, which also have a kiddy corner with a video running, toys, and scaled-down rockers or benches to keep children occupied while you shop. You can also earn "Gymbucks" during specific weeks: For every $50 you spend you'll get a $25 coupon that will be good during a specific upcoming period of time, both in stores and online (gymboree.com).

Hanna Andersson Fans of this Swedish brand swear by its comfort (the absolute softest organic cottons you'll ever encounter) and durability; Hannas tend to last from kid to kid. In fact, the catalog and website invite you to share your stories about your most long-lasting Hannas. There are a few signature Hannas for babies, including one-piece "Zippers" and "Wiggle Pants"—designed to fit over diapered bottoms without bunching and bagging. Hannas come in European sizes, but both the catalog and website (hannaandersson.com) have charts that make it easy to figure out what to order for your baby based on his weight and length. You'll pay more for Hanna Andersson clothing, but you'll get a lot more wear out of it; and if you sign up to receive the catalog and e-mail notices of sales, you can get some amazing bargains when things get marked down. Hanna Andersson stores are starting to pop up slowly in some malls in major cities (hannaandersson.com).

Zutano This line of children's clothing features particularly darling coordinates for newborns (one-piece outfits, tops, bottoms, and hats that you can mix and match), in super-soft cotton and bright, fun prints. If you have a preemie, check out their Itzy Bitzy line, which is especially designed to fit babies weighing between 4 and 8 pounds. A pretty floral kimono top is $18; pull-on pants to match are $10 (comfykids.com).

▼ ZUTANO'S PLAYFUL PATTERNS IN COORDINATING COLORS HELP YOU MAKE A MINI FASHION STATEMENT.

KEEPING IT ALL CLEAN

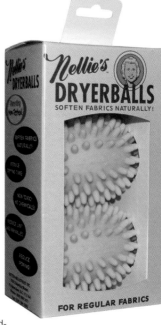

BABIES AND TODDLERS can get pretty messy. You'll be amazed at how much laundry one little kid can generate (and the loads increase exponentially as your family expands). Here are some tips for cleaning your baby's clothes, plus the products you'll want to stock up on:

◆ **Detergents** Scan the laundry aisle at your supermarket and you'll see that there are detergents labeled just for babies. Are they necessary? Maybe, maybe not. What sets these products apart is that they lack dyes and harsh cleaning agents that can leave irritating residues. **Dreft** is a popular choice; it claims to be specially formulated to get out baby-specific stains like spit-up and urine and to rinse away thoroughly so no residues are left behind (about $10 for 100 ounces). **All** makes a detergent that's formulated for babies; it's less costly ($30 for two 200-ounce bottles). But any laundry detergent that contains sodium lauryl sulfate or sodium laureth sulfate should be gentle enough to wash your baby's clothing in.

◆ **Fabric softeners** As with detergents, choose one that's scent-free; same goes for dryer sheets. However, don't use fabric softener on clothing that's labeled "flame resistant," such as sleepwear. The fabric softener may dilute the fabric's flame resistance.

GIZMOS & GADGETS

Keep your baby's wardrobe wrinkle-free with **Nellie's Dryerballs.** These spiny spheres bounce around in the dryer, fluffing clothes as they go ($20 per pair, Batten Industries).

◆ **Stain removers** Every kind of baby stain presents a special challenge, from your newborn's spit-up to your toddler's melted chocolate ice cream. The key to getting out any kind of spot is to treat it as soon as possible. When you're at home, remove stained clothing right away, rinse with cold water to dilute the stain, and then spritz with a stain treatment that you can leave on, such as **Spray 'n' Wash** or **Zout,** until you have time to do laundry. Or, you can toss it into the washer to soak; before you add in the rest of the laundry, get rid of the soaking solution by running the washer through a rinse cycle.

◆ **Laundry enhancers** Relative newcomers to the laundry aisle, these products claim to help get clothes cleaner than detergent alone, thanks to soil dispersing. One brand that's really taken off is **OxiClean,** which comes in a "free" version—meaning it has no bleach, harsh chemicals, dyes, or scents, and won't leave a residue on clothing ($6.50 for 64 ounces). OxiClean also makes a number of baby-specific products, including a stain removal spray ($5 for 22 ounces) and a soaking solution ($4 for a 1.5-lb tub).

◆ **Laundry sorters** Some moms like to do their baby's laundry separately from the rest of the family's, at least for the first few weeks or months. It's not necessary, but if you like using a strong, scented detergent on your own clothes, you might want to do your baby's duds separately, using a gentler product, to avoid the risk of irritating his delicate skin. To cut down on laundry basket clutter, invest in a divided sorter like the **BetterBasket,** a soft-sided organizer with two sets of handles and three compartments, making it easy to tote several batches of separated clothing to the laundry room and back ($25; betterbasket.com). Another space-saver: **Stack n' Sort Laundry Baskets** ($11 each, Rubbermaid). They can be assembled vertically while full, or nested together while empty for storage.

Mom Tip!

"I wash my baby's socks in a mesh laundry bag so they don't get lost in the laundry room shuffle."

3
FEEDING

HOW AND WHAT you feed your baby will change many, many times over the course of her first few years—and the gear you'll need to keep her nourished will evolve as well. Here's a quick, basic checklist of feeding must-haves. Once you've digested the rest of this chapter, you'll discover that there are other things you might want or need:

If you plan to breast-feed: nursing bras, nursing pads, nipple cream, breast pump, breast milk storage bags, bottles, and nipples so others can feed your baby

If you plan to bottle-feed: bottles, nipples, formula

When your baby starts solids: a high chair, baby spoons, bibs

When she starts feeding herself: sippy cups, toddler utensils, plastic bowls and plates

When you're on the go: portable snack containers and cups

When she outgrows her high chair: a booster seat

The good news, especially for the faint of wallet, is that you don't have to buy all this stuff at once—and some of the big-ticket items (high chair, breast pump) you may be able to borrow. The most important thing to remember about mealtime: What matters much more than gear and gadgets is that your child has an opportunity to bond with you (and others). When you nurse your baby or look into her eyes as you give her a bottle, when you place her high chair near the table while the rest of the family sits down to eat, you nourish her mind and soul as well as her body.

BOTTLES & NIPPLES

WHETHER YOU FEED YOUR BABY formula, nurse her, or do both, you'll need to lay in a supply of bottles and nipples. When shopping for these items, keep in mind that your baby might have the final say—she may well prefer one type of bottle or nipple over another and if so, will let you know in no uncertain terms! So don't buy in bulk until you know what works for *your* child.

BOTTLES

What to consider when choosing your bottle brand:

◆ **Capacity** Your newborn will only take in 2 to 3 ounces of formula or pumped breast milk every 2 to 4 hours, so you may want to buy a few smaller, usually 4- or 5-ounce, bottles to use in the beginning. It'll save you space in the cupboard until your baby starts taking bigger meals, around 3 months; then you'll need a supply of larger capacity bottles (8 or 9 ounces).

◆ **Plastic versus glass** It's still possible to buy glass bottles, but their fragility and weight (imagine toting several around in a diaper bag!) make them the least desirable choice. Still, some moms prefer the perceived purity of glass. (For the record: if the concern is about chemicals in plastic products, there have been no reported problems with the plastics used to make baby bottles.) That said, Evenflo makes clear glass bottles in 4- and 8-ounce sizes (about $6 for a pack of 3).

◆ **Appearance** Some bottles come in tints or have designs on them. Whatever you choose is a matter of taste—yours and your baby's. An older baby who's refusing to take a bottle for some reason might be enticed by one that features a cute animal or familiar object.

◆ **Shape** Besides the classic baby bottles, you'll see angled ones (so a baby can be fed in a semi-upright position, which helps prevent fluid from flowing into the middle ear) and hourglass-shaped ones—the idea being the inward curve creates a natural grip for your baby, who will be able to hold her own bottle at around 6 months.

◆ **Burp-busters** Most popular baby bottles claim to prevent air from entering a baby's mouth while she nurses—the point being that swallowed air is what causes painful gas. This is achieved in a variety of ways; the jury's out on whether any one is better than another, meaning trial-and-error will be your best guide.

▼ THE VELCRO STRAP OF THE PODEE BOTTLE INSULATOR ($7) FASTENS THE BOTTLE TO A SAFE PLACE (THE BEAR IS DETACHABLE).

▲ THE SPLASH DRYING RACK ($30; SKIPHOP.COM) IS A GOOD STORAGE SOLUTION FOR BOTTLES AND NIPPLES, AND LOOKS COOL TO BOOT!

◆ **Reusable versus disposable** The former can be popped into the dishwasher and used over and over again. The "disposables" actually refer to plastic liners that are fitted into a reusable plastic holder. These are often called "nursers" rather than bottles, and some claim to help prevent gas because they "collapse" as a baby nurses; moms sometimes prefer them because they make cleanup easy, although some moms complain that they leak.

◆ **Cost** Name-brand bottles are comparable in price. Expect to pay from $9 to $14 for a 3-pack of most styles and sizes. You may save a little per bottle with a "system," "starter," or "gift" pack, which, depending on the brand, may include several bottles in different sizes, extra nipples, a bottle brush, and more. But if the extras aren't items you want, you're better off just buying the specific bottles and nipples you know that you'll use.

◆ **Hassle** Some bottles have more pieces than others, so you'll have to assemble and reassemble the bottles, wash each piece individually, and risk losing parts. This inconvenience may be worth it if the multipart bottle is the only one that seems to keep your baby from getting too gassy. And, of course, if you choose a disposable bottle system, you'll be faced with continually having to stock up on liners.

Here's a rundown of the most popular bottle brands and what they have to offer. Most can be found at baby stores, big-brand stores, drugstores, supermarkets, and online. Many moms and babies tend to be brand-loyal, but choosing the best bottle is very subjective.

Avent

◆ The reusable **Avent Natural Feeding Bottle** comes in 4-, 9-, and 11-ounce sizes; claims to reduce colic; curves inward in the middle for an easy grip; and comes with a clear-plastic lid that fits over the nipple for portability.

◆ **Avent's VIA Nurser** features hard plastic liners that can be reused up to three times before being tossed and can be used to store breastmilk. The nipples are compatible with both the bottle and nurser.

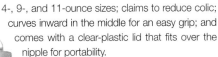

◄ AVENT BOTTLES CONNECT TO THE AVENT MANUAL PUMP.

GIZMOS & GADGETS To prevent all those bottle bits and pieces (including nipples) from getting lost in the dishwasher, put them in a plastic dishwasher basket designed to keep them all contained on the top rack.

61

Playtex

◆ The **VentAire Bubble Free Bottle** is angled and available in 6- and 9-ounce sizes, as well as four pastel colors. There are a variety of nursers, which all take **Drop-Ins Pre-Formed Soft Bottle Liners**: these include the **Premium Eazy Feed Nurser** (8-ounce only), and the **Premium Designer Nurser** (which comes in six designs; 4 and 8 ounces).

Dr. Brown's Natural Flow

◆ These reusable bottles feature a two-piece contraption (a vent and a vent reservoir, which can be purchased separately if needed to replace lost or worn ones) that fits inside the bottle to prevent air bubbles. They come in standard and wide-neck versions, and in 2-, 4-, and 8-ounce sizes. "These were a godsend," says one mom, " especially when formula was rough on my baby's tummy."

Evenflo

◆ **Classic Clear** bottles, **Classic Light Tint** bottles, and **Classic Decorated** bottles—which come in 4- and 8-ounce sizes—include the **CustomFlow** nipple, which responds to the pressure of a baby's sucking.

◆ **Comfi** bottles are angled and sport a non-slip grip and elliptical shape to make holding them easy; they come in 6- and 9-ounce sizes.

◆ The **Elan** bottles feature a one-piece vent system to prevent bubbles, a silicone nipple with textured and raised areas to help with latch-on, and are compatible with the Evenflo Elan breast pump; also in 6- and 9-ounce sizes.

Gerber

◆ Basic reusable bottles come in a 2.5-ounce size (for preemies), as well as 5- and 9-ounce sizes, and in clear, tinted, and decorated styles.

◆ **GentleFlow** bottles have wide mouths and come in a 9-ounce capacity only.

◆ **ComfortHold** bottles are triangular in shape to make them especially easy to hold.

Soothie

◆ The nipple on this bottle is fashioned after the same Soothie pacifier used in hospitals; lots of babies prefer this particular "plug" over any other (see page 65 for more

▲ THE WIDE MOUTH ON THE GERBER GENTLE FLOW BOTTLE MAKES CLEANING THEM EASIER.

about pacifiers). Besides the special silicone nipple, the 5- and 9-ounce Soothie bottles come with a convenient bottle cover that snaps onto the bottom so it won't get lost.

Second Nature

◆ The nipple on this bottle has tiny holes that open as a baby sucks: The stronger the pull, the greater the flow. These come in a 9-ounce size only ($13 for a 3-pack; onestepahead.com).

Sassy

◆ **MAM** bottles come in 5- and 9-ounce sizes, and in "boy" (blue and green) and "girl" (pink and yellow) colors.

Podee

◆ This unique baby bottle consists of a bottle and nipple connected by what looks like a long, flexible straw. The idea is that it allows for feeding in an upright position, thought to help reduce air bubbles and even ear infections ($9 for one 8-ounce bottle; babiesrus.com). It was a favorite for one mother in our survey who said, "The Podee self-feeding bottle system was extremely helpful for my twins. I could feed both of them at the same time, hands-free."

▲ THE HANDS-FREE BOTTLE FROM PODEE GETS SPECIAL KUDOS FROM MOMS OF MULTIPLES ($9).

NIPPLES

Nipples are made of latex, silicone, or rubber. Latex (which is tan in color) is soft and flexible, but not as durable as the other materials. Rubber is soft and long-lasting, but less flexible. Silicone nipples are firm, hold their shape longer than rubber or latex ones, and aren't damaged by heat when boiled; they're also clear and are the more expensive of the three.

$KIP, $AVE, OR $PLURGE?

You can spend a tiny bundle on a contraption that will steam-clean bottles, nipples, pacifiers, and such—we've seen bottle sterilizers for as much as $90 (that's enough to cover dinner out, a movie, and even a babysitter!). But tossing those things into the dishwasher and setting it on "heated drying" will kill germs just as effectively. So will boiling them for a few minutes on top of the stove. Save the bucks for date night.

Mom Tip!

The key features to consider when choosing nipples:

◆ **Compatibility with the bottles you like** Not all nipples will work with all bottles; in fact, most nipples are bottle-brand-specific. That means that you may well be choosing a bottle and nipple together. But that's okay: There are tons of options out there, so you're bound to find a single bottle/nipple brand that works for you and your baby.

◆ **Shape** If you're planning to both nurse and bottlefeed your baby, look for a nipple with a wide base that gradually tapers down to the tip of the nipple (much like the shape your breast takes inside your baby's mouth). Otherwise anything goes as long as your baby seems happy with it.

◆ **Angle** A nipple that leans to one side automatically tilts into a baby's mouth and can make feeding easier.

◆ **Venting** A small hole in the neck of the nipple lets air into the bottle while keeping liquid in, so the nipple doesn't collapse. This is rarely an issue, however; most babies keep the nipple erect by opening their mouths as they nurse to let air back into the bottle.

GIZMOS & GADGETS

Using powdered formula? Two items that simplify mixing: **Shake N Serve Formula Pitcher** (by Babies 'R' Us; $8) lets you measure, cover, then shake formula and water, and store it in the fridge. **Avent's Formula Dispenser and Snack Cup** ($6) and **Sassy's Powdered Formula Dispenser** ($5) each have single-serving compartments for powder that can also convert to snack holders.

NIPPLE SHAPE	WHAT IT DOES
Standard nipples (long rounded tip)	Easy for most babies to suck from
Orthodontic nipples (flat on the top)	Go further back into a baby's mouth, much like a mother's nipple and breast would release milk further back in the baby's mouth, presumably making it easier for her to swallow
Tri-cut nipples (longer than standard ones)	Supposed to elongate if the baby opens her mouth wide enough and sucks hard enough to pull it into her mouth. (If you're breastfeeding, this type of nipple could interfere with good latch-on habits)
Nubbin nipples (short, flattened tips)	Sometimes more difficult for the baby to grasp, especially if the baby is also breast-fed

$KIP, $AVE, OR $PLURGE?

While there's no health reason a baby's formula or milk needs to be warm for her to enjoy and be nourished by it, many moms prefer heating their babies' bottles. And breast milk comes out warm, so some breastfed babies may prefer having their bottled meals heated. But this can easily be done by placing the bottle into a bowl full of hot water, or running a bottle under a hot tap. There's no need for a bottle warmer, which can set you back as much as $45—and if you're like a lot of the moms in our survey, you'll wind up shoving it into the back of cabinet. **NOTE:** Don't ever, ever put your baby's bottle into the microwave to heat it. The liquid will heat unevenly, and may present a scalding hazard.

PACIFIERS

Mom Tip!

"I bought a dozen of my son's favorite pacifier (the NUK) and kept them everywhere—in the diaper bag and the stroller, in every room of the house, in coat pockets, etc. That way I could always get my hands on one in a hurry."

BABIES ARE HARDWIRED TO SUCK—and not just in order to eat. It soothes them, which is why so many pair a pacifier or thumb with a blankie or other lovey: The combo is comforting. Not all babies take to a pacifier, and those who do are often quite picky about their "plug"; they'll only accept a certain kind. So don't worry about getting your baby to take a pacifier or choosing the "right" one if she does. If you offer her a few, most likely she'll pick the one she likes—or spit them all right out of her mouth.

That said, there's plenty of variety among pacifiers. Some features you'll find:

◆ **Nipple material** Pacifier nipples are made of either silicone or latex.

◆ **Nipple shape** Many pacifiers claim to be "orthodontic," meaning they won't interfere with the proper growth and development of a baby's mouth, teeth, or jaw. **Gerber's NUK** pacifiers ($4 for two) are a popular orthodontic paci.

◆ **Nipple size** Most pacifiers will be labeled according to age (for babies 0 to 6 month, 6 months and up, and so on).

◆ **Ventilation** To cut down on irritation around the mouth (where saliva can gather under the sides of the pacifier), many feature holes or other openings.

◆ **Style** Pacifiers come in all sorts of colors and designs. One fun option: The fancy-looking **Munchkin Bling pacifier** ($5).

◆ **Hospital "grade"** The plain-Jane **Soothie** paci given to newborns in the hospital has something of cult following: Some babies won't take anything else ($5).

◆ **Cover** Some pacifiers come with a little plastic case, but we love the **Keep-It-Kleen** pacifier, which has shields that close over the nipple when it leaves the baby's mouth ($5).

▼ NOT BORN WITH A SILVER SPOON IN HER MOUTH? THERE'S ALWAYS THE MUNCHKIN BLING PACIFIER ($5).

BREAST PUMPS

IN MANY WAYS, BREAST-FEEDING is as primal and simple as it sounds; there's no special equipment required beyond a well-rested, well-nourished, always-accessible mom. That said, there's gear that can make nursing easier for everyone, which is good, since it's well established that breast-feeding for at least the first year is one of the best ways to keep your baby healthy for a lifetime. Here is a rundown of the basic supplies you'll need for breast-feeding and how to choose among them.

BREAST PUMPS

A good pump is a nursing mom's best friend. It allows her to:

◆ pump and store milk when she and her child are apart.

◆ keep up her milk supply when her baby sleeps through a meal or isn't eating well. (Breast milk supply hinges on demand: The more a baby nurses, the more milk is produced; the less she nurses, the less milk that's produced).

◆ relieve engorged breasts.

◆ take a break from some nighttime nursing sessions by letting her set aside milk that can be bottle-fed by Dad.

◆ establish her milk supply if she has a preemie who's too small and weak to nurse at first.

There are a lot of options when it comes to pumps. The one you choose depends mostly on how you'll use it: If you're going to be returning to work full-time, you may want to rent or buy a double-setup electric pump, with adjustable speed and suction levels; pumping both breasts stimulates them to produce more milk (and saves time). But if you just need a break at home or have more flexibility at work, a hand pump may be fine. Your selection will also depend on which you feel most comfortable using and which allows you to pump the most milk most efficiently. Here's what you should know about each type of pump:

HOSPITAL-GRADE RENTAL These are the fastest and most efficient, but they're heavy and unwieldy—not practical for travel or the office. Most moms opt for this type of pump when they have a preemie or an infant with feeding problems. You might also consider renting one if you're not sure you want to breast-feed and therefore aren't ready to spend money on your own pump. The hospital where you deliver your baby can point you in the direction of a lactation

GIZMOS & GADGETS

The **Easy Expression Bustier** lets you pump sans hands, plus it zips up in front for easy access. ($30; Easy Expression Products)

Mom Tip!

"I kept a borrowed breast pump at my office, and purchased one for home. That way I didn't need to tote the pump home at night or on weekends—I just carried the milk and bottles back and forth in an insulated bag."

66

consultant or business that rents pumps; it'll probably run you from $1 to $3 per day, plus around $60 for a personal accessory kit.

MANUAL PUMP With this simplest and least expensive type of pump, suction is generated when you squeeze a lever. Manual pumps are lightweight, super portable, and don't require an electrical outlet. They're also very quiet. On the downside, manual ones aren't always as efficient as electric models, and you can only pump one breast at a time.

ELECTRIC PUMP A high-quality electric pump is the best choice for long-term daily pumping (some moms prefer to pump milk and bottle-feed, rather than nurse) for moms who work outside of the home. Or, if they have a generous milk supply, some moms pump and store so their babies can continue to enjoy the benefits of breast milk even after they've weaned. Most models allow you to pump two breasts at once, feature variable speeds and suction, include bottles, tubing, and other necessities, and come in an easy-to-carry (though not necessarily lightweight) case.

THE CHOICES

Here are some specific models and the reasons why moms love 'em:

◆ **Medela Pump N Style** This is a favorite among electric pumps for working moms. It comes in several versions, starting at about $130. One of the most popular is the **Pump N Style Advanced,** which features separate let-down and expression modes, a rechargeable battery so you can pump when they're no outlets around, and comes in either a shoulder bag or backpack case ($350; medela.com).

◆ **Avent Isis Manual Pump** Once the milk lets down, many moms find they don't have to squeeze the lever as many times as other manual pumps to keep the flow going; plus, they can pump directly into the baby's bottle—and the entire thing is dishwasher-safe ($45; avent.com).

◆ **Gerber Massaging Manual Breast Pump** A manual pump that combines two sets of pads to massage nipple and areola; it's dishwasher safe and easy to assemble ($40; gerber.com).

▲ AVENT WILL SEND REPLACEMENT PARTS (FOR A FEE) IF YOU LOSE OR DAMAGE A PIECE OF THE PUMP.

GIZMOS & GADGETS
Rather than store pumped breast milk in bottles, stock up on special storage bags. These are pre-sterilized and designed to be labeled with permanent marker. (Put the date and amount of milk in each bag, especially if you're laying in a supply of frozen milk before you go back to work; you'll want to use the oldest milk first.) Breast-milk storage bags are usually marked like measuring cups, in ounces; some are designed to flatten at the bottom when filled, so they can be neatly arranged in the fridge or freezer.

GIZMOS & GADGETS

To sterilize breast pump parts, pop them into a **Quick Clean Micro-Steam Bag** by Medela, add water, and zap in the microwave for 3 minutes. They'll come out steam-cleaned and ready to air-dry ($5 for 5 reusable bags—each can be used up to 20 times).

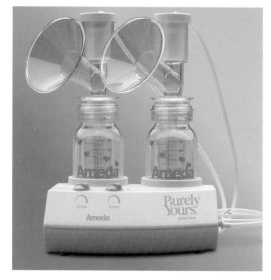

◄ FOR MOMS WHO HAVE A HARD TIME PRODUCING MILK, ELECTRIC PUMPS LIKE THE AMEDA PURELY YOURS ($200) ARE A BETTER OPTION THAN A MANUAL PUMP.

◆ **Playtex Embrace** Its suction action is designed to mimic how a baby's mouth stimulates milk flow. It has five speeds and five suction levels, super-soft cups, and comes in a black totebag with labeled pouches for easy storage ($249; playtexbaby.com).

◆ **Ameda Purely Yours** It weighs just one pound, features eight suction levels and four speeds, and also works with three different power sources (AA batteries, electricity, and car adapter, which is included). It comes in a tote bag or backpack. ($200; amedababy.com)

◆ **Isis IQ Duo** This pump can be set to match the speed and suction level that you find most comfortable, and that most closely resembles that of your baby. You start by manually pumping, then the machine sets itself to match. Its modern design makes it the most attractive pump ($350; avent.com).

Mom Tip!

"To avoid spills when transferring just-pumped milk to a storage bag, I first place the bag inside of a glass; that way it stays upright as I fill it. I've never lost a drop!"

$KIP, $AVE, OR $PLURGE?

Is it okay to borrow a breast pump? Purists will say no, but the truth is, if you invest in your own tubing, cups, and bottles, borrowing the machine itself should be fine. For reasons of intimacy, it may be the kind of thing you'd borrow from your sister, but not necessarily a colleague from work. Just make sure you get the right stuff. Some brands of replacement tubing and the like are available in stores, but some brands, such as Medela, you may have to purchase from a lactation consultant or company, online, or even from a hospital that provides breast-feeding support (most do).

SOME THINGS THAT WILL MAKE breast-feeding more effective and comfortable for you and your baby:

NURSING BRAS These are a must. Your bigger-than-usual breasts will need the support, and you'll want to be able to access them as quickly as possible when your baby announces, at full volume, that it's snack time. Although you'll be tempted to stock up on nursing bras before your baby's born (you'll want at least three—one to wear, one for the wash, and one to have clean and on hand to change into in case of serious leaks), this can be tricky: It's hard to predict just what size you'll need until your milk comes in fully. Ask for guidance at your favorite maternity store; to be on the safe side, buy just one nursing bra to get you started. Besides size, consider the following features when bra shopping, and expect to pay from $30 to $40 for a good-quality bra:

◆ **Fabric** Soft, breathable cotton is the most comfortable and healthiest choice.
◆ **Underwire** This will provide the most support, especially for breasts that become very heavy.
◆ **Strap configuration** Straps that form an "X" in the back (like a sports bra) also give extra support.
◆ **Openings** Some bras open at the top of the cup and fold down; others open in the middle and fold out. Which is best is a matter of personal preference.
◆ **Type of closure** Whether the bra has snaps or a hook-and-eye (the most typical), make sure that it opens and closes easily—with one hand.
◆ **Style** You may want to invest in a nursing sports bra if you're active, as well as a sleep bra (these have soft cups that are easily pushed aside for nursing).

NURSING BRA PADS Slip one inside of each bra cup to absorb embarrassing leaks. You can buy disposable ones, or washable cotton ones.

BREAST SHELLS These ventilated plastic domes fit over sore nipples to allow them to air dry (when you can't go bra-less) and prevent bra fabric from rubbing against them. One type to try: **TheraShells Breast Shells** ($10; Medela).

NURSING ACCESSORIES

NIPPLE CREAM Moms swear by the healing power of the pure lanolin in **Lansinoh** ($10 for 2-ounce tube). Go ahead and stock up: It works wonders on chapped, cracked lips as well.

NURSING PILLOW Look for one that's firm enough to support your baby in a horizontal position (this will help her latch on correctly) and that brings her to your nipple level, like the C-shaped pillows made by Boppy. The **Boppy Infant Support and Feeding Pillow** ($35 with washable cover) wraps around your waist: While your baby stretches out on one side, you can lean your elbow on the other. The moms in our survey raved about how these made nursing easier and more comfortable, and also loved that they could use the pillow in other ways—to help support a just-sitting-up baby or as a prop for tummy time. Also by Boppy: the **Boppy Nursing Pillow,** which has a panel of fabric within the "C" to support a baby's weight ($35). Other nursing pillow features to look for: a removable, washable cover and, if you're concerned about appearances, fabric styles that can coordinate with the nursery.

Mom Tip!

"I bought two nursing pillows—one for upstairs and one for downstairs: It saved countless trips up and down!"

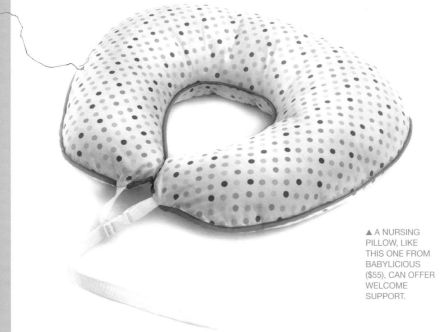

▲ A NURSING PILLOW, LIKE THIS ONE FROM BABYLICIOUS ($55), CAN OFFER WELCOME SUPPORT.

CUPS

GIZMOS & GADGETS

Are you a sippy cup loser? Turn your luck around with **Take & Toss 7-Ounce Spill Proof Cups.** These brightly colored cups are durable enough to use over and over again (they're dishwasher- and micro-wave-safe), are beautifully simple in design (just a cup and lid—no other small pieces to misplace), and cheap enough to be disposable (or lose-able) ($12 for a pack of 24; The First Years).

MOST BABIES ARE READY to move from a bottle to a cup at 1 year (which is when pediatricians recommend making the switch to whole milk from formula). Many moms don't adhere to this advice, which is fine, but even if you don't give up the bottle altogether, 12 months is a good time to introduce a cup and to start serving him water and juice (in limited amounts) from it. It'll make weaning from the bottle easier down the road, when your baby is ready. Nearly all the bottle makers, from Avent to Sassy, Playtex to Gerber, also offer cute, well-made sippy cups that are available everywhere from drugstores and supermarkets to baby stores and online. Some features to look for:

◆ **A soft nipple** This can make the transition easier for a reluctant sipper. One to try: **Avent Magic Cup** ($8 for two 9-ounce cups).

◆ **A good grip** Two handles are better than one. **Gerber's Transition Cup** has handles that can adjust to three different positions ($6).

◆ **Spill-proof design** Most sippy cups are spill-proof; just look for the words on the label. Also choose a cup that has a valve inside to prevent liquid from leaking out of the spout; these can be a pain to keep track of and to clean, but are worth the trouble. (And you can easily pick up spares at your supermarket or drugstore.)

◆ **Insulation** A cup like **Munchkin's Insulated Spill-Proof Trainer Cup** ($10 for two 9-ounce cups) will keep beverages chilled for hours.

◆ **Kid appeal** Most sippy cups come in bright colors or feature designs, like cartoon characters, making them more likely be used. A toddler who has mastered sipping can move on to slurping with a cup that has a straw—and you'll love it when she does: It means she can handle milk in a plastic, lidded cup at a restaurant (no more toting a special cup for her!).

◀ INSULATED CUPS, LIKE THESE FROM MUNCHKIN (ABOUT $20 FOR FOUR), CAN MAKE HOT DAYS COOLER.

71

BOWLS, PLATES, & UTENSILS

WHEN IT'S TIME TO INTRODUCE SOLIDS—pediatricians now urge parents to wait until a baby is at least 6 months old (because she's able to sit up by herself and less likely to gag and because she's less likely to develop allergies if you wait), you'll want to invest in flat- and tableware that can accommodate a tiny mouth now, and tiny hands soon (most kids are ready to try feeding themselves at around 12 months). What you'll need:

BABY SPOONS

Look for a first feeding spoon that:

◆ **has a long handle**

◆ **sports a small bowl**

◆ **features a soft, rubbery bowl** to protect tender gums if your baby suddenly decides to bite down. It will also serve as an effective "squeegie" for scraping pureed peas off a little chin.

◆ **includes a temperature indicator,** which can help prevent burns: the bowl of the spoon will change colors if the food is too hot.

◆ **is dishwasher safe** Sure, it's fine to use that sterling silver baby spoon from Aunt Martha for your baby's very first bite of mashed banana, but after that, stick with spoons that don't require special care. You'll have your hands full cleaning up your baby, her high chair, the floor, and your own outfit after meals.

GIZMOS & GADGETS

To help your baby enjoy foods she can't yet chew, give it to her in a little mesh bag that she can gum to her heart's content. She'll get the nutrients and juice from, say, a section of orange, but not big bits to choke on. **2 + 2 Baby Safe Feeder** includes two feeders and two replacement bags—all of which can go in the dishwasher ($11; Designs 2-U).

UTENSILS FOR SELF-FEEDERS

By the time she's 12 to 14 months old, your child will have the fine motor skills needed to grasp a spoon, the large motor skills required to scoop up food and bring it toward her mouth, and the hand-eye coordination to get it there. At around 18 months she can try using a toddler fork. To make this all as easy as possible for her, look for utensils with the following features:

◆ A toddler spoon with a small bowl, preferably plastic (for comfort) that's not too shallow (so any food she manages to scoop into it stays put), like those made by **Baby Bjorn** ($9 for two)

◆ A toddler fork with short, rounded prongs (for safety reasons)

◆ Utensils with easy-to-hold handles. Look for short, fat, textured grips, looped handles, and other innovations

◆ Temperature indicator (optional): A fork or spoon that changes color when food is too hot, like **Munchkin's White Hot Spoon and Fork** ($3.50 for both)

◆ Kid-appeal, like **Gerber's Glitter-Filled Fork & Spoon** ($4 for the pair)—utensils with fun colors and designs are more likely to be used

GIZMOS & GADGETS

Can't remember how long that half-full jar of puréed peas has been in the fridge? Next time you have unfinished food, suction a **Digital Day Counter** on the lid—it'll keep track of how old the food is. Just remember, don't save any food that you've put a spoon in that's also been in your baby's mouth ($10 for two; Days Ago).

▼ MUNCHKIN WHITE HOT SPOONS HAVE A FLEXIBLE TIP THAT'S EASY ON THE GUMS ($3.50).

TABLEWARE FOR SELF-FEEDERS

▲ BOWLS THAT CAN'T BE OVER-TURNED, LIKE THESE MUNCH-KIN STAY-PUT BOWLS ($15), MAKE CLEAN-UPS MUCH EASIER!

No matter how well your baby has mastered the art of feeding herself, you're still years away from breaking out the fine china. Instead, serve your child in plates or bowls that:

◆ **are shatterproof.** That means melamine or plastic.

◆ **won't slip and slide.** This could mean a rubber bottom, or one that will stick to the high-chair tray or table. We like **Stay-Put Suction Bowls by Munchkin** ($15).

◆ **won't tip easily.** For example, the thick, molded plastic and wider-at-the-base design of **Baby Bjorn's Toddler Plate** ($20 for a bowl, spoon, and fork in yellow, green, or red) makes it nearly impossible to flip over (the rubber bottom helps too).

GIZMOS AND GADGETS

For no-spill snacking when you're out-and-about, put a stash of crackers, cereal, or other favorite finger food in a plastic, lidded container designed for nibbling on the go. We like the **Snack-Trap** ($5; Made for Mom): Your baby can easily reach inside the soft, slotted top, but the treats won't fall out of it.

74

GIZMOS & GADGETS

With solids comes the risk of choking—but it's one you don't have to worry about as long as you stick to foods that are developmentally appropriate for your child's age (go to parenting.com for guidance). Make sure that what you feed her is of a consistency that she can handle. In the beginning, that means mashed to a pulp when it comes to just about anything. The back of a fork will do just fine for most soft fruits like bananas and very, very ripe pears, and for well-cooked veggies like sweet potatoes. For everything else, stick to jarred baby food, or put everything into a mill. One we like: **Kidco's BabySteps Basic Natural Feeding System** ($12; kidco.com for stores). It has two freezer storage trays and comes with a recipe book.

◆ **are deep enough to make scooping food easy.** Even plates should have molded sides that slant upward.

◆ **divides and conquers.** That is, it divides the peas from the potatoes, and conquers food phobias. For kids who hate it when their food touches, opt for a plate that has separate sections.

▶ THE GREAT DIVIDE: A PLATE WITH SECTIONS, LIKE THIS ONE FROM GERBER (ABOUT $5 FOR TWO), CAN APPEASE PICKY EATERS.

75

GIZMOS & GADGETS

Babies and toddlers will eat as much straight off the table as they will from their plates or bowls, so if restaurant germs worry you, keep a stash of disposable placemats in your diaper bag, like **Table Toppers** ($10 for 20; neatsolutions.com), or **Doodle Diners** (also $10 for 20; safetybuddy.com). Both have adhesive strips to keep the mats in place, and colorful, kid-friendly designs.

◆ **makes short work of cleanup.** Bowls or plates that come with lids let you skip the tedious step of scraping leftover pasta into a separate container. For instance, the **Toddler Feeding Set by Tommee Tippee** ($7 for bowl, spoon, and fork) features not just a lid, but also a compartment for stowing the utensils for on-the-go meals.

◆ **won't offend your mealtime aesthetics.** If once in a while you'd like to set a table that's attractive to you but still kid-friendly, you can find some terrific-looking unbreakable dinnerware. Try **French Bull,** which makes children's place settings in mod, colorful designs ($20 for plate, bowl, cup, and utensils), or **Pottery Barn Kids** ($30 for a set of 4 sectional melamine plates in assorted solid colors). Specialty baby stores often carry lovely dinnerware for kids.

"I use paper cupcake wrappers as snack holders. They fit perfectly in my kids' little hands, and cleanup is easy—I just toss 'em."

◀ FRENCH BULL PLACE SETTINGS ($20) ALLOW YOU TO SET A GREAT-LOOKING BABY-PROOF TABLE.

76

Mom Tip!

"I spread out an old plastic shower curtain under my baby's high chair to catch all the dollops of food that would otherwise land on the floor."

THIS IS ONE TOPIC the moms in our survey had especially strong opinions about—and for good reason: As one respondent says, your child will be in her high chair at least three times a day, so it's best not to skimp on quality. Beyond that, you'll want to make sure the seating you choose has the right bells and whistles for you both.

HIGH CHAIRS

Features to consider when shopping for a high chair:

◆ **Ability to recline** A chair that can be tilted back in one or more positions can make it a great place to keep a young baby who's not yet eating but may be able to hold her own bottle: She can snack on that or take a nap in the kitchen while you cook. A chair that's labeled "from birth to 45 pounds" (or so) will last you for quite some time—at least until your child refuses to sit in it any longer.

◆ **Height adjustability** You can raise or lower the chair to the perfect height for spoon feeding, or to the same level as everyone else at the table.

◆ **Wheels** In our survey, high chairs with wheels got yays—and those that didn't got nays. It's easy to see why: Wheels let you move the chair from spot to spot. Look for wheels or casters that swivel, and make sure they have a locking mechanism.

◆ **Washable seat pad** A vinyl one can be cleaned easily with a disinfecting wipe; be sure you can get between the pad and the actual seat of the chair as well—bits of food like to get trapped under there.

▼ THE CENTER BAR IN THIS GRACO HIGH CHAIR ($99) PROVIDES AN ADDED LEVEL OF SAFETY FOR SQUIRMY BABIES.

◆ **Appearance** You can find more and more chairs in solid colors and simple, sophisticated designs that may look more like they belong in the dining room than in the nursery.

◆ **Adjustable footrest** This can accommodate your baby's growth.

◆ **Stowability** In a small kitchen, a chair that you can fold and stash away will be a boon.

◆ **Removable tray** Your child will eat as much directly off the tray as she will from her bowl, so you'll want a tray that you can clean thoroughly between meals. One that will fit in the dishwasher is a bonus; if you can remove it with one hand, that's a double bonus!

◆ **Cup holder and other tray compartments** This accommodates sippy cups and snacks.

◆ **A secure restraint system** A 3-point seatbelt is ideal.

77

▶ THE FISHER-PRICE SPACE SAVER HIGH CHAIR ($50) IS AN EXCELLENT OPTION IF SPACE IS AN ISSUE.

◆ **Storage space** Not a must, but you may appreciate having a bar to hang bibs on and/or an compartment for stashing toys—particularly if space is at a premium in your kitchen.

◆ **Activity tray or toy bar** Until your child gets bored with the playthings included, this will save you a lot of dashing around looking for something to keep her happy in the chair for just five more minutes—until the pasta's done!

◆ **Simplicity** If you want a high chair that's, well, just a high chair, check out the ultra-plain **Antilop by IKEA** ($19). It's made of white plastic with metal legs and doesn't even come with a tray; you buy that separately ($5). Note that the chair does have a seat belt, but it just goes across the lap, making it not an ideal restraint for very young babies or for those old enough to try to climb out. Also consider a simple, old-fashioned wooden chair, but keep in mind that it won't be comfortable without some sort of padding (which you'll have to launder often) and may not feature a good restraining system. **Eddie Bauer** makes a number of wooden models—one mom described hers as "inexpensive, easy to clean, and attractive."

◆ **Versatility** Combi's **Transition High Chair** converts to a toddler table and chair ($130).

◆ **Price** Expect to spend from about $70 to $150 for a name-brand high chair.

▲ IKEA'S ANTILOP HIGH CHAIR ($19) IS SITTING PROOF THAT BASIC CAN BE BEAUTIFUL.

$KIP, $AVE, OR $PLURGE?

High-end high chairs that convert to a booster seat, then to a chair for an older child are appealing for their versatility and seeming longevity. But they're pricey; for example, the **Tripp Trapp** by **Stokke** is $200 (and you have to buy a cushion separately), and the **Svan** (at egiggle.com) is $235. Both have quality construction, but their ultramodern design is not for everyone. And if you truly want to get your money's worth, you'll be looking at them in some form or another for at least the next 13 or 14 years. On the other hand, both are designed to be pushed right up to the table and can safely and comfortably sit a child as young as 6 months old.

▲ EASY FOLDING:
FISHER-PRICE'S
HEALTHY
CARE BOOSTER
SEAT ($25)

BOOSTER SEATS are a great second seating option (you can buy one for grandma's house or even keep one in the trunk of the car), though many parents will use a booster seat in lieu of a high chair. If kitchen space is tight, a sturdy booster seat with secure restraints will do the job of a high chair while taking up far less room. Booster seats also come in handy during that transitional period: When your child is about 2 years old and is starting to get a bit big for the high chair, but can't quite see over the top of the table without a little... boost. Versatile and inexpensive (most booster seats are in the $20 range), they're a handy piece of gear to have around. Here are the things you should consider when choosing one:

◆ **Safety** Make sure the seat will stay put on a kitchen or dining room chair. This can be achieved with a no-tip design and/or straps that secure the booster to the chair. Since all chairs are different, make sure you can return the booster you buy if it turns out to not be compatible with your furniture.

▲ PORTABLE BOOSTER SEATS, LIKE THIS ONE FROM SAFETY 1ST ($15), ARE GREAT FOR ON-THE-GO DINING.

◆ **Height** The chair should elevate your child enough so that she can eat comfortably at the table, with room for her legs under the table.

◆ **An eating tray** If you'd like your child to keep the mess she makes of meals off the dining room table, put her in a booster that has a separate tray. **Safety 1st's Easy Care Swing Tray Booster** ($15) features a tray that simply swings open—no struggling to attach or detach it.

◆ **Easy cleanup** The fewer nooks and crevices for crumbs and other food particles to get caught in, the better. Look for a booster with parts that are dishwasher safe, like the **Fisher-Price Healthy Care Booster** ($25).

◆ **Stowability and portability** A lightweight booster seat that folds up compactly can be stashed in a closet or toted to a restaurant or Grandma's house.

◆ **Clamp-on seats** These boosters attach to the table rather than sit atop a chair (which is one advantage right there, especially if you're short on seating). They usually consist of strong fabric on a sturdy steel or aluminum frame, are lightweight, and collapse easily. They're the perfect second booster to have on hand for travel or dinners out. One to check out: **Easy Diner Portable Hook on High Chair by Regalo** ($20), which has a five-point safety belt and removable, washable seat pad. (The clamps cannot be adjusted on this seat, so it might not fit on some tables.)

▼ REGAL LAGER'S CLAMP-ON BOOSTER SEAT ($50) FOLDS UP FLAT, SO IT CAN BE STORED IN A STROLLER BASKET.

PLACE MATS & SPLAT MATS

▲ THE FISHER-PRICE MIRACLES & MILESTONES TABLE TOP PLAYMAT ($15) FOLDS UP SO YOU CAN TAKE IT WITH YOU FOR ON-THE-GO MEALTIMES.

WHEN IT COMES TO PLACE MATS FOR KIDS, your goal isn't simply to protect the table from crumbs and goo—you also want to entertain them so that they'll sit in one place for as long as possible. Look for mats with fun pictures or that your child can draw on with chalk or washable marker: like the **Wacky Packy** mat by Arte Bebe ($13). On one side it's an elegant, easy-to-clean mat featuring a friendly elephant; on the other it's a blank surface for doodling with markers. We also love the **Piggy Platter Placemat** ($25, Smarty Parents): It's a clear mat that your child can slide a picture into and admire while she eats; plus, the mat's rounded rims contain spills, and it's dishwasher-safe for easy cleanup.

Splat mats are large squares of plastic or laminated fabric that you spread beneath your child's seat to protect the floor from crumbs. On tile or hardwood floors they may be more trouble than they're worth (what's so tough about sweeping?), but if you have carpet a mat can be a lifesaver. Look for one that's at least 40 by 50 inches square and is easy to clean.

BATHTIME

SPLISH, SPLASH, IT'S TIME FOR A BATH!** Depending on your baby's age and stage of development, this can be really challenging for both of you, or the most fun you'll have together all day. Many infants are soothed by a warm soak in the tub, and older babies love to play in the water. Toddlers also enjoy the fun part, though many balk at the washing-up part (especially being shampooed).

What you need to know and have on hand to make tub time easy for you, safe and comfortable for your baby, and a treat for all, starting with some bathing basics:

You don't need to bathe your baby every day. Until your newborn's umbilical stump dries and falls off, you'll be giving him sponge baths every other day or so. In between he'll be fine with daily gentle wipe-downs with a clean warm wash cloth in key spots (the diaper area, his neck, chin, and cheeks where drool and spit-up collect, and between his tiny fingers). Same goes for older babies who've moved on to the big tub, but once your baby can sit up and play in the water, you may want to bathe him every day for the sheer delight of watching him splash and explore. Toddlers, who can get pretty grimy while eating and playing, may need to be bathed daily as well.

When you bathe your baby is your choice. Some parents like to make a bath part of the morning routine, to give their child a fresh start to the day. Others prefer to run a tub in the evening. Many moms swear by a bath an hour or so before bedtime to help a child of any age get to sleep more easily. It will bring his body temperature up slightly—and when it drops, this induces sleep. Two not-so-great times to stick a baby in the tub: When he's hungry and right after he's eaten, when he's likely to spit up from being jostled around.

SAFETY FIRST

FOR BABIES UNDER 1, bathtubs are even more dangerous than swimming pools: They're the No. 1 cause of drowning. A baby under water can lose consciousness in 2 minutes, and suffer permanent brain damage in 4 to 6 minutes. Plus, a quarter of all serious scalds in kids 4 and younger happen in the tub. There are various products designed to protect babies and toddlers during a bath, but they won't do any good unless you're vigilant about the following:

◆ Turn the thermostat on your hot water heater down to 120°F (25°C) to prevent scalding.

◆ Never leave your child's side. (Even kids up to age 8 shouldn't be unattended in the tub!)

◆ Only fill the tub a few inches when bathing your baby—and fill it *before* you put him in.

◆ Keep the edge of the tub (or kitchen sink if you bathe your baby in the kitchen) free of sharp and/or dangerous objects like razors.

GIZMOS & GADGETS

Don't have time to sit around and watch the tub fill? Stick the **Shower Pets Starfish Bath Sensor** ($15; showerpets. com) to the inside of the tub at the desired height and it'll beep when the water reaches it. That way you can walk away and not worry that the tub's going to overflow while your gather towels, toys, and, oh yes, your tot. (It's also a temperature gauge.)

GIZMOS & GADGETS

The **Baby Bath Gate** is a safety gate for the tub: It creates a barrier between your baby and the hot faucet and fixtures, and pops out easily when it's your turn to soak ($30; thebaby-bathgate.com).

INFANT BATHTUBS range from very simple styles to fancy models that come complete with their own showerheads! (See "Skip, Save, or Splurge" below.) What you choose depends on which bells and whistles, if any, appeal to you, how much space you have, and what you feel like spending on an item that you'll use at most for six or seven months: A baby tub can cost as little as $10 and as much as $40. Some features to look for:

◆ **A back that reclines** just enough to keep the baby semi-upright.

◆ **A shape that conforms to her body** A molded tub that has a little dip where the baby's bottom goes and a little rise to support her legs behind the knees will be most comfortable for her and help keep her from slipping out of position. (Even so, you'll need to keep an eye and a hand on her at all times.)

◆ **A layer of foam** along the back of the tub, to provide a soft, non-skid surface.

▼ THE FISHER-PRICE AQUARIUM BATH TUB ($30) GROWS WITH YOUR BABY UNTIL HE'S READY FOR A BIG TUB.

$KIP, $AVE, OR $PLURGE?

Several companies are turning out infant tubs that come with a spray attachment, but they're pricey—as much as $40—and the sprayers don't tend to work very well. As one of the moms in our survey said of hers, "No matter how many times I changed the batteries, the sprayer never worked. The water would only trickle out." The bottom line: A plastic pitcher or cup is just fine for rinsing.

◆ **A drain with a plug**

◆ **Convertibility** Some tubs are designed to recline for infants, and then adjust to accommodate older babies. One mom in our survey loved her **Summer Newborn to Toddler Bath Center** (about $30): "It grew with my baby, and she's still using it after a year." Another versatile option: the **Aquarium Bath Tub** by **Fisher-Price**, which features a mesh hammock that can be reconfigured within the tub to accommodate a baby at different stages. At $30 it's a higher-end option, but you get a lot of splash for your bucks: The tub comes with three toys, including one that has a thermometer for testing water temperature.

◆ **Portability** A simple mesh sling that fits in a sink or tub is a lightweight alternative to a hard, molded plastic tub. Check out **Mother's Touch Baby Bather,** which folds flat for easy storage ($15; Summer Infant). For older babies who can sit up in the tub, try a blow-up model that can be deflated for storage or travel. The **Snug-Tub** features suction cups so you can attach it to the bathroom tiles to dry (about $20, Kelgar). This and other blow-up tubs are a good option from about 6 to 12 months, at which point many babies start to get too big for them.

▼ BECAUSE IT TAKES LESS WATER TO FILL UP THAN THE BATHTUB, THE SNUG-TUB DELUXE FROM KELGAR (ABOUT $20) IS A GOOD OPTION FOR CONSERVING WATER.

GIZMOS & GADGETS

Bath seats, meant to help keep a baby upright in the water, create a dangerous false sense of security: The seat can tip over, trapping your child under water. Bath seats have gotten such bad press that they're hard to find, but if someone offers you a used one, pass it up. A freebie isn't worth the risk.

◄ FOLD-UP TUBS LIKE THIS ONE FROM SAFETY 1ST ($9.99) CAN BE STOWED UNDER THE SINK WHEN NOT IN USE.

◆ **Stowability** Some fold up for easy stashing. **Safety 1st's Space Saver Fold Up Tub** is a full-size tub, with a reclining backrest and drain plug, that folds to half its size ($9.99).

◆ **Convenience** If you like having everything at hand, look for tubs that have a place to hold a bottle of body wash or shampoo. The **Comfy Bath Center** from **Safety 1st** ($13) has an accessory tray for soap, shampoo, and a pitcher for rinsing.

◆ **Temperature strip** Many tubs, such as the **Comfy Bath Center** from **Safety 1st** and **Summer Infant's Rite-Temp Baby Bathtub** ($19.99), come with a built-in temperature strip so you can make sure your infant's bathwater falls safely and comfortably between 90 and 100°F.

$KIP, $AVE, OR $PLURGE?

Your baby's tub is one item you should buy new (his potty seat is another). A tub that's been used by another child has no doubt been peed and pooped in several times over and may still harbor bacteria, especially in the foam backing. At about $20, a new tub is worth the peace of mind.

87

A QUICK DUNK, and then you're done… if only it were that easy! In fact, besides your baby's tub, there are lots of items to help make bathtime easier, safer—and more fun. Some that we (and the moms in our survey) especially like:

A PLACE TO REST YOUR WEARY BONES If you've spent any time kneeling on the cold, hard floor of your bathroom, you know how uncomfortable it is—especially on your knees, elbow, and back. There are a number of contraptions designed to take the pressure off:

◆ **Infantino's TubSider**
While it looks like something you might find in the gym, this innovative product fits on the side of the tub and provides both an angled seat and knee and elbow pads for support while kneeling. It adjusts to most tubs, and folds for storage (about $40).

◆ **Safety 1st Tubside Kneeler and Step Stool** Scoot this clever two-in-one item next to the tub to protect knees and elbows. Converts to a stool for your child ($15).

▲ YOUR KNEES AND BACK WILL APPRECIATE THE TUBSIDER FROM INFANTINO (ABOUT $40).

BATH TOY STORAGE What to do with all those toys while they dry off—besides leaving them scattered in the tub? Some smart storage solutions:

◆ **Mesh bags Alex** makes one that comes with suction cup hooks that you mount on the tile wall of the tub; fill the bag with wet toys, then hang to dry ($9).

◆ **Boon Frog Pod** has a detachable scooper that lets you gather, drain, and store wet toys in one fell swoop ($30).

◆ **Fisher-Price Corner Bath Cubby** This soft-sided cubby has a cute fish motif, suction cups to attach it to a corner of your tub, and a mesh bottom to allow toys to drain. One drawback: The fabric is prone to mildew, so it may require regular trips to the washer ($9).

▲ BOON'S FROG POD ($30) ALSO HOLDS BOTTLES OF BATH PRODUCTS, SO EVERYTHING'S IN ONE PLACE.

Mom Tip!
"I drape a towel over the edge of the tub so it's more comfortable to lean my elbows on. Comes in handy when my baby starts to splash, too!"

Mom Tip!

"I taught my toddler to howl at the moon while I rinse his hair: He loves tipping his head way back and yowling for as long as it takes me to get the shampoo out."

GIZMOS & GADGETS

Keeping little kids' nails clean can be a challenge (just wait till your tot discovers lime green Play-Doh!), but these cute critters make it easier: The **Wett Giggles** animal-topped nailbrush comes nestled in a bar of gentle soap. ($10; wettgiggles.com)

SHAMPOO HELPERS One day your baby doesn't mind if you pour water over his head; the next day, suddenly, the party's over and he freaks every time you attempt to wash his hair. When most kids reach this stage, they're still too young to understand the concept of tilting their heads back and closing their eyes. In the meantime, you can hand your little protestor a fresh washcloth to hold over his face, or just grit your teeth and rinse. Or try one of these gadgets moms swear by:

◆ **Swim goggles** Any brand will do; in the summer you can pick up a pair of baby-size goggles at the drugstore for a few bucks. Just make sure they fit tightly enough to keep the water out.

◆ **Bath visors** These foam visors (which can also be used in the sun) keep little faces dry and also keep shampoo out of your child's eyes. Two we like: **One Step Ahead's Shampoo Visor** (5.95 for two; onestepahead.com) and the **Bath and Sun Visor** from **Sassy** ($6 for two)

◆ **Shampoo Rinse Cup** This little pitcher has a soft, flexible edge that forms a watertight band against your baby's forehead so water can't drip into the eyes ($8.99, rightstart.com).

▼ SAFE SUDS: THE BUBBLE DUCKY SPOUT GUARD FROM MUNCHKIN ($10)

Mom Tip!

"To keep my 18-month-old's hands busy while I wash him up, I give him a soft toothbrush so he can 'help' by scrubbing his arms and legs."

FAUCET COVERS Many a little noggin has gotten bumped on the sharp protruding edge of a tub tap. A foam "sleeve" that fits tightly over it can help prevent this from happening. Two options:

◆ **Soft Spout Cover by Safety 1st** It's inflatable for extra protection (about $5).

◆ **Munchkin's Bubble Ducky Spout Guard** This cute cover dispenses bubbles and fits most standard faucets ($10).

FUN IN THE TUB

RUBBER DUCKIES have their charms, but there are a lot of toys competing for tub time these days. When shopping for things for your baby to play with in the bath, keep in mind:

◆ Squirt toys get moldy inside, and are impossible to clean. Skip 'em.

◆ Avoid toys with small parts or pieces that could come off easily and make their way into your baby's mouth.

◆ Crayons, paints, and other "art supplies" make more of a mess than they're worth. Save finger painting for dry land.

◆ Choose toys that fit easily in little hands. A plaything that's too big for your baby or toddler to hold and manipulate easily spells frustration—not fun. This is especially true for things that are meant to fill up with water: They'll get heavier when full.

◆ A toy that looks too much like a drinking cup will tempt your baby to drink his bathwater—yuck! Try to pick playthings that look like, well, playthings.

Mom Tip!

"I give my baby a clean paintbrush during his baths. He loves 'painting' designs with foamy soap all over the wall!"

TYPES OF TOYS TO LOOK FOR:

◆ Toys that will help your baby experiment with the properties of water: things he can fill and pour from, and have sieves that allow water to flow through

◆ Boats that really float

◆ Aquatic creatures that bob and float in the water. **Sassy's Counting Fish 'n' Net** toy ($7) comes with fishies and a net, for instance.

◆ Terry cloth bath puppets (these can double as washcloths, meaning your child might be more compliant when it's time scrub up)

◆ Shapes, letters, and numbers that stick to the side of the tub. We like the funky set of bath toys by **Boon,** which includes three balls, two mini-scrubbers, and 15 colorful appliques that float, stick to the side of the tub or the tile wall, and are mold-and-mildew resistant ($14).

◆ A doll that's meant to go in the tub; your child will love washing up his own little baby.

▼ BATH GOODS BY BOON ($14) INCLUDES TWO MINI MESH SCRUBBIES WITH THE BATH TOYS.

BABY BEAUTY ESSENTIALS

THERE'S NOTHING SWEETER-SMELLING than a baby fresh from the tub, but be careful what you put on your child's delicate skin and scalp. Some things to keep in mind when considering your little one's toiletries:

◆ **Harsh soaps** can irritate brand-new skin, so choose a mild body wash or soap and use it sparingly, especially if your baby has a rash. (Soap your baby at the end of bath time, so he's not sitting in suds for long periods while he plays.)

◆ **Just because a product has "baby" on the label,** doesn't mean it's gentle. In general, products for infants are formulated to be free of additives, but don't go by the label alone. For example, that sweet scent might be irritating to your child's skin.

◆ **Grown-up products** labeled for "sensitive skin" are often fine to use on your baby, but be aware that these usually don't have the "no-tears" formula found in many children's soaps and shampoos.

◆ **Limit the variety of chemicals** you put on your baby's skin. Look for products with as few ingredients as possible.

◆ **An unscented cream** or lotion is best for babies with dry skin, especially those prone to eczema (red, scaly, itchy patches). It should be slathered on right after bath time, while skin is still damp.

◆ **Limit the bubbles.** Prolonged exposure to the perfumes and dyes found in most bubble bath formulas, as well as the chemical that creates the bubbles, sodium laureth sulfate, can break down the skin's natural barrier to infection, causing redness and swelling in both boys and girls. When the skin around a little girl's vagina is affected, she could develop symptoms similar to those of a urinary tract infection, or an actual UTI. Look for bubble bath products without perfumes and dyes, and little or no sodium laureth sulfate (it shouldn't be one of the first three ingredients). Don't give your child a bubble bath more than once a week.

◆ **Baby powder isn't necessary.** It won't protect against diaper rash (to find out what will, see page 106).

◆ **Make it easy on yourself.** Look for pump bottles—there's less spillage, no screw tops to fumble with, and you can use them one-handed.

MOMS' FAVORITE BATH PRODUCTS
SOAPS AND BODY WASHES

◆ **Aveeno Essential Moisture Baby Bath** The moisturizing oatmeal and soy in this product make it an especially good choice for dry skin ($4).

◆ **Johnson's Bedtime Bath** This lavender and chamomile body wash has a dreamy scent that will help your baby wind down for bedtime ($3). Johnson's also makes a rosemary, eucalyptus, and menthol-scented bath (**Vapor Bath**) that can help ease a stuffy nose ($5).

◆ **Huggies Natural Care Baby Wash** Extra Gentle Formula is a treat for sensitive skin ($3).

◆ **Mustela PhysiObebe** A no-rinse cleanser (just smooth it on, then wipe it off with a cotton ball); it also softens and moisturizes ($14).

◆ **Cetaphil** Though not a baby product per se, this ultra-gentle cleanser can be rinsed off or wiped off and leaves behind a thin layer of moisturizer ($10).

Mom Tip!
"My kids hate it when I put lotion on them after a bath because it's always cold. So while they're in the tub, I put the lotion bottle in the water with them, and it's warm when they get out."

▲ MUSTELA PHYSIOBEBE ($14) IS HYPO-ALLERGENIC, SO IT WILL NOT IRRITATE DELICATE SKIN.

93

▲ A MASSAGE BEFORE BEDTIME WITH LOTION SUCH AS GERBER'S GRINS AND GIGGLES ($4) CAN MAKE FALLING ASLEEP MUCH SMOOTHER.

Mom Tip!

"I use a baby wash that's made for both hair and body: I can clean my daughter from her hair on down with one big dollop."

LOTIONS AND CREAMS

◆ **Gerber Original Baby Lotion** It's made with oatmeal, a proven moisturizer ($4).

◆ **Aveeno Calming Comfort Baby Lotion** This gentle lotion contains oatmeal, which soothes dry, itchy skin; its delicious scent—lavender and vanilla—soothes frazzled nerves ($4).

◆ **Baby Magic Gentle Baby Lotion** This tried-and-true brand is dye-free and hypoallergenic ($3).

SHAMPOOS

◆ **Johnson's Baby Shampoo** The only thing that's changed about this original "no-tears" shampoo since you were a kid (it's still soap-free, alcohol-free, and hypoallergenic) is that it now comes in several different varieties, including lavender-scented (relaxing before bed) and in a creamy "softwash" formula ($6 for 20 ounces).

◆ **Johnson's Extra Conditioning and Detangling Shampoo** One mom in our survey reported that this shampoo alone was as effective at getting out knots as a detangling shampoo and conditioner combined.

GROOMING

Yes, we know, your child's already a head-turner, but he'll still need to be groomed. Here's what you'll need to help your pretty baby keep up appearances:

HAIR CARE Whether your infant was born with a full head of hair or mere wisps, you'll want to keep it neat. Brushing will also distribute oils on the scalp, which can help control cradle cap—a common condition among newborns in which excess oil build-up translates into unsightly flakes. Choose a brush with the softest of bristles; you can find inexpensive ones at the drugstore or supermarket.

NAIL CARE Too-long nails can scratch delicate baby skin and get dirty underneath. If you prefer scissors, look for a pair that has rounded points. If you find clippers easier to use, opt for ones with blades that are sized for tiny fingers and a grip that is big enough for you to control easily. We like the **American**

GIZMOS & GADGETS

Dispense with the soap dispenser altogether: Johnson's Baby Head-to-Toe Washcloths get sudsy when wet. They're especially great for travel, because they're disposable ($4 for 14).

▼ A NAIL CLIPPER WITH A MAGNIFIER, LIKE THIS ONE FROM FIRST YEARS ($5), WILL HELP YOU CLIP YOUR BABY'S NAILS WITH CONFIDENCE.

Red Cross Care Nail Clipper with Magnifier ($5; The First Years); a magnifier makes it easier to see those tiny nails as you snip them.

TOOTH AND GUM CARE Many pediatric dentists advise wrapping a piece of sterile gauze around a finger and running it along your baby's gums. Seems like overkill to us, but as soon as that first pearly white pops out, you'll want to start getting your child used to having a brush in his mouth.

◆ **You can buy a soft silicone or rubber device** like **Baby's 1st Toothbrush** ($10 for two) that curves around each tooth and has tiny little bumps that gently scrub off food debris.

◆ **If you opt for a real toothbrush,** choose one that's specially made for tiny mouths (meaning it'll have a small head) and has the softest possible bristles. Many feature kid-friendly designs, like cartoon characters, on the handle, which can help to entice a reluctant child to open wide. (You'll be doing the brushing until he's at least 5 or 6, and even after that you'll be supervising.)

◆ **Toothpaste** Brands with fluoride are not recommended for kids under 2, who'll probably swallow toothpaste rather than spit it out. (Excess fluoride can actually weaken and darken teeth.) Although toothpaste isn't necessary for getting teeth clean, it doesn't hurt to try a fluoride-free one, like **Oral B Stages Tooth and Gum Cleanser** (about $3) and **Orajel Toddler Training Toothpaste** (about $3); both taste good, so your child might be more willing to let you brush. Once a child can swish and spit, you can move on to a regular toothpaste or choose one just for kids that tastes like bubblegum or fruit.

▼ ORAJEL'S CHILD-FRIENDLY TOOTHPASTE FLAVORS CAN MAKE BRUSHING LITTLE TEETH FUN FOR BOTH OF YOU.

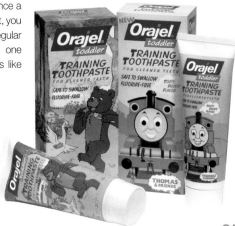

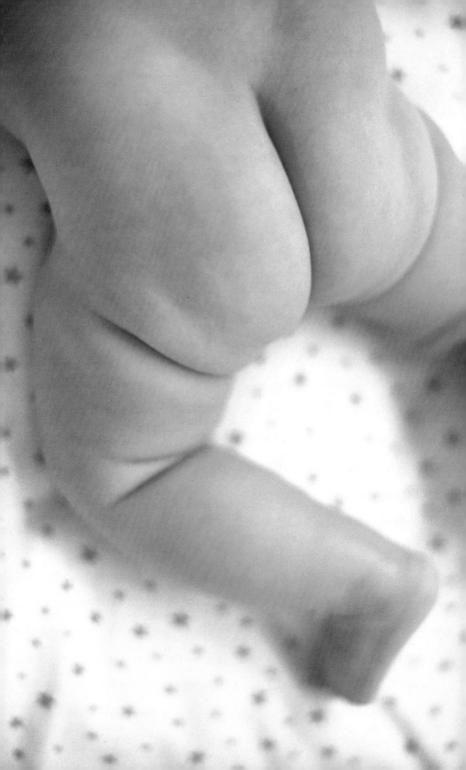

5
BOTTOMS UP

Wavering between disposable diapers and cloth ones? Perplexed about the vast array of baby wipes you see in the drugstore? Can't decipher the ingredients list on a tube of rash cream? Diapering a baby isn't exactly rocket science—but when you're new at it, figuring out how to care for your baby's flip side can be confusing. To help you make informed decisions about everything from which brand of disposable will be best for your child to how to size up a potty seat, we've got you (and your baby's bottom) covered.

DIAPERS

WHEN IT COMES TO COVERING your baby's bottom, you'll need to make two big decisions: First, will you use cloth diapers or disposable ones? And second, especially if you choose the latter, which brand and style will you buy?

What to consider when deciding between cloth and disposable diapers:

◆ **Diaper rash** There was a time when cloth-clad babies had fewer rashes than their disposable-diapered peers, but because modern disposables wick moisture away from skin, this idea no longer holds water. And studies have found that disposables reduce the incidence of infection in group settings, so if your child is going to be in daycare, it may be best to go with disposables. (In fact, the center may require that you use throwaways.)

◆ **Comfort** Disposables are cut to fit a baby's bottom like a glove, and many sport other feel-good features like stretchy sides that help guarantee a snug fit and soft, cloth-like material. But the newest cloth diapers also come in fitted shapes (no more bulky triangular folds).

◆ **Convenience** There's no question disposables are the more user-friendly option, but cloth diapers have made some big improvements in this area, with Velcro closures (no need for pins) and removable linings. Add in the fact that you don't even have to wash them yourself—you can send cloth diapers out to be cleaned—and they're practically as fuss-free as disposables.

◆ **Expense** Ultimately, you'll spend roughly the same amount on disposables and cloth diapers (about $700 the first year!), if you choose to have the latter laundered by a diaper service. You'll save a little bit by washing cloth diapers yourself. (A little bit of money, that is; given that a new baby goes through about 10 diapers per day, you certainly won't save any time!)

◆ **Environment** Disposables consume resources when they're manufactured and pile up in landfills after they're used (they're about 40 percent biodegradable). Washing cloth diapers uses energy and water, and leaves behind dirty water that your city must clean. Neither option is really more "green" than the other.

DISPOSABLE DIAPERS

The differences between brands are minimal. Most rely on the same technology to absorb moisture and wick it away from a baby's sensitive skin, though many moms find they prefer one brand over another after a little trial and error and stick with it.

A key thing to consider when assessing a disposable diaper is fit. If it's loose or saggy, if the leg openings don't gently hug your baby's thighs, if the waistband can't be adjusted to fit snugly around her belly, then you're going to have leaks no matter how absorbently high-tech the diaper is. Make sure you've got the right size on your baby or try a different brand.

The diaper's ability to wick moisture away from a baby's skin is equally important. When you change a wet diaper, your child's skin shouldn't feel damp; if it does or if you're dealing with constant diaper rash, consider switching to another brand.

Mom Tip!

"To keep my 18-month-old still while I change him, I let him scribble on paper I tape above his changing table. He doesn't even notice what I'm doing!"

Keep these criteria in mind when you try any of these brands of disposables:

PAMPERS This is probably the best-known national brand of disposable diaper. **Regular Pampers** come in two sizes: **Swaddlers** (for the first five months) and **Cruisers** (with stretchy sides and a trim fit around the legs for older, mobile babies). **Baby Dry Pampers** come in six sizes (to fit babies from 8 to 35-plus pounds) and cost a little less than the brand's other styles.

HUGGIES The other big-name disposable offers two main varieties of diaper: **Huggies** and **Huggies Supreme** (the former less expensive and more basic, as in not as stretchy or streamlined in terms of fit); both come in sizes 1 through 6 for babies up to 35 pounds. There's also a newborn diaper that features a cutout in the front of the waistband to accommodate a healing belly button and a super-absorbent overnight diaper for older babies.

LUVS This national brand comes in one variety and six sizes and costs a bit less than the competition. Some of the moms in our survey felt that Luvs actually fit their babies better than the more expensive brands.

STORE BRANDS Many large chain stores—from pharmacies like CVS and more general stores like Target and Wal-Mart to supermarkets like Kroger and Safeway—carry their own line of disposable diapers. Because they're usually less expensive than the national brands, they're worth trying if you want to save money. They may not always feel as soft as a pricier brand, and they won't sport, say, a licensed character logo (Pampers, for instance, are adorned with Sesame Street characters). They may vary in terms of how absorbent they are, so if you wind up changing your baby more often when she's wearing a certain kind, or if you're dealing with lots of leaks, try another kind.

CLOTH DIAPERS

To wrap your baby's bottom in cloth, you basically have two options: buying your own supply of diapers and laundering them yourself, or using a diaper service.

If you opt for buying your own cloth diapers, you may need to do a little shopping, since cloth diapers aren't as readily available as disposables. They're sold online—one of the moms in our survey swears by the **Bummis** brand ($145 for a cotton diapering starter kit that includes 36 cloth diapers, 6 wraps, and a roll of liners)—and baby stores like Babies 'R' Us, BuyBuy Baby, and Baby Depot all carry at least one brand of cloth diaper. Figure on buying at least 30 cloth diapers for a newborn or young baby; you can cut that number to about 20 once your child is older.

GIZMOS & GADGETS

A diaper caddy, like the **Skip Hop Toolbox Caddy,** below, ($38; skiphop. com) can really help cut down on changing-table clutter. It holds up to a dozen diapers and has two side pockets with room for an assortment of creams, ointments, and cotton balls. The drawers (accessible from either side) hold other diaper-change essentials and keep them close at hand. The caddy has a built-in handle and can be moved from room to room.

Some features to look for when shopping for cloth diapers:

◆ **A contoured shape,** much like a disposable—this means that when the diaper is laid out flat it has an hourglass shape, narrower in the middle to fit comfortably between a baby's legs.

◆ **Elasticized legs,** to make sure the diaper fits snugly enough to prevent leaks.

◆ **A "hook-and-loop" closure,** so the diaper fastens with Velcro or something similar rather than a safety pin.

◆ **Adequate absorbency** For example, one of the most popular brands of cloth diapers, **Kushies** ($50 for a pack of five), has five layers of cotton flannel, a middle "soaker" layer, and a waterproof outer layer (which means there's no diaper cover required).

◆ **Optional inner liners** These are washable, contoured layers of cotton that can be inserted into a cloth diaper when extra protection is needed (at naptime or overnight, for example).

▼ KUSHIES ULTRA DIAPERS (ABOUT $8 EACH) HAVE A WATERPROOF OUTER LAYER, SO NO DIAPER COVER IS NEEDED.

102

◆ **A variety of sizes.** Kushies come in four sizes, from preemie (for babies weighing between 2 and 4 pounds) to toddler (for kids up to 45 pounds). **Dappi Cloth Pinless Diapers,** ($4 apiece) come in three sizes, fitting babies up to 24 pounds or more.

A diaper service can be a great option if you want to use cloth. How much the service costs depends on how often you use it and where you're located. Generally, diaper services run $50 to $80 per month. For your money you'll get:

◆ **Convenience.** The service will wash your baby's diapers, pick up the soiled ones, and deliver a batch of clean ones—typically on a weekly basis. All you have to do is plop your baby's soiled (unrinsed!) diapers into a special hamper provided by the service and have it ready at pick-up time. You don't even have to be home.

◆ **Super-clean nappies.** Diaper services use thirteen changes of water and high-temperature drying that eliminates bacteria.

◆ **The right number of diapers for your child.** When you sign up, the service will help you figure out how many diapers to start with. After that, you'll receive as many fresh diapers each week as you turn in dirty ones.

◆ **The option to rent or buy diaper covers.** These go over the diaper and eliminate the need for pins.

GIZMOS & GADGETS

A diaper stacker is a tent-shaped hiding place for diapers, in the event your changing table doesn't have ample storage or you just don't want to look at diapers on open shelving. Many bedding manufacturers now offer coordinating diaper stackers in the $15-$20 range. They're a good bet if you want to stock up on diapers (most can hold several packs) and down the line can have a second life holding soft toys or small articles of clothing. But if you've already got shelving or another place for diapers and wipes, a stacker is definitely not a must-have.

DIAPERING SUPPLIES

YOU'LL NEED A FEW MORE THINGS to keep your baby's bottom clean and dry—and to make every change as easy as possible for you.

WIPES

The evolution of baby wipes has followed much the same trajectory as that of disposable diapers: First there were just a few major brands with few variations—and then there were all sorts of types of wipes, as well as a plethora of copycat store brands. Some things to consider with baby wipes:

◆ **Scent** The perfumes in scented wipes may irritate a baby's sensitive skin; if you find that's the case, stick with unscented ones. You can go a step further and opt for wipes that are made especially for sensitive skin (usually labeled "hypoallergenic").

◆ **Texture** Some wipes are smooth; others have a rippled texture. The latter may clean poop residue more effectively, especially that of older babies who've started eating solids. A larger, thicker wipe will certainly clean better than a thin, flimsy one. This is where you'll find differences between brands, especially between national brands and store brands; the latter will be less pricey, but may work just as well—or it may not. One of our survey respondents bluntly warned: "Generic wipes aren't worth the money!" But we found just as many moms were disappointed with some brand-name wipes—"Too stiff!" and "They dry out too fast." If a brand or type doesn't work for you, try another.

◆ **Added ingredients** You can find wipes with aloe or shea butter, meant to help keep skin soft (as if a baby's bottom is ever anything but!), or with lavender or chamomile, meant to be calming. They tend to cost the same as the plain products, but whether they achieve what they claim will depend on your baby. Just make sure if you try a wipe with something added that it doesn't bother your child's skin.

◆ **Packaging** You'll probably find that you want to use more than one of these options in order to meet your needs:

1) Hard plastic tubs They're convenient and reusable, designed to keep wipes from drying out. Pop-up boxes, similar to tissue containers, are becoming increasingly popular and sophisticated: Many also feature buttons that open the lids. Just be aware that tiny hands can get stuck in the openings, so watch your baby around the wipes container.

104

2) Refills These are cheaper (and more eco-friendly) than tubs, and you can use them whether or not you've already bought a plastic tub. They're usually resealable so the wipes don't dry out between changes. They're especially convenient anytime you have to squeeze them into a small space, like a suitcase.

3) Travel packs You can find hard plastic containers that hold full-size wipes but are about the thickness of a datebook. These are refillable and fit nicely inside a diaper bag, the glove compartment or backseat pocket of a car, or the storage area of a stroller. Also available and cheaper, are similarly-sized soft packages of baby wipes, but these can't be refilled.

◆ **Flushability** Most baby wipes should not be flushed down a toilet. There are a number of flushable wipes for toddlers and older kids on the market, but these may not be gentle enough to use on a newborn—and besides, you'll rarely be next to a toilet when you're changing your baby. If you do have a child who's potty training, however, a flushable wipe could be a godsend. Not only are they more effective than plain toilet paper, so that your little "Me do it!" munchkin will be more likely to get herself clean, they're packaged to appeal to kids—meaning they'll be more likely than other products to get used. Flushable wipes usually come in refillable, pop-up tubs. Some we like are **Kandoo Flushable Toilet Wipes** by **Pampers** ($4 for 50; they come in three kid-friendly scents) and **Cottonelle Kids** by **Kleenex** ($4 for 42).

Mom Tip!

"I keep an extra, stocked diaper bag in the trunk of my car, and at Grandma's house, my best friend's house, and anywhere else I spend a lot of time."

Mom Tip!

"Before I toss dried-out wipes, I try a little warm water—it will bring them back to life."

$KIP, $AVE, OR $PLURGE?

A baby wipes warmer may be a luxury worth passing on. While you might cringe at assaulting your baby's behind with a cold, damp wipe, the truth is, he's not going to mind. Plus, as one mom says, "I really thought the wipes warmer was a great idea, but then the wipes would always dry out or burn on the bottom—what a waste!"

RASH CREAMS

The variety of diaper rash creams is endless. Here's what to consider when choosing:

◆ **Active ingredient** The best rash creams work by forming a barrier between a baby's skin and moisture. Zinc oxide, the main ingredient in white creams, does an excellent job. Generally, the thicker the cream, the more zinc oxide and the more protective it is, but a heavy concentration of zinc oxide makes the product sticky. If your baby doesn't have a rash, try a lighter formula, like **Balmex Creamy Lotion Barrier** or **Desitin Creamy.** Even when your baby doesn't have a rash, it's good to create a barrier between his skin and the diaper. Some moms find that plain old petroleum jelly, like **Vaseline** ($4), does a fine job of protecting skin. If your baby has a serious rash, **Triple Paste** (about $9 for a 2-ounce tube) almost always clears it up right away. **Aquaphor Healing Ointment** is also a bit pricey (about $8 for 3.5 ounces), but it's great for everything from red bottoms or chapped cheeks to your own dry spots.

▲ TRIPLE PASTE KEEPS WETNESS FROM IRRITATING YOUR BABY'S SKIN AND CAN BE USED DAILY TO PREVENT DIAPER RASH OUTBREAKS ($9).

◆ **Extra ingredients** **Palmer's Bottom Butter** ($4) contains cocoa butter. **BabyADE Rash Cream** ($6) helps heal with vitamins A, D, and E. And **A&D Diaper Cream** ($6.50) has aloe—said one mom fan: "My baby has never had a diaper rash. Amen!"

◆ **How it's applied** Most rash creams come in a squeeze tube, but others are designed to make application easier—like **Petkin's Rash Stick** ($5).

◆ **Name brand vs. store brand** Find a rash cream that you like, and it may well be that Target or CVS or your supermarket makes a similar product that's cheaper. Just compare the ingredients list on both, and if they're the same, go ahead and try the store brand. The packaging may not be as cute, or it may not have the same scent, but it will most likely perform as well as the pricier version.

GIZMOS & GADGETS

While many parents like trash bags (scented or not) for collecting soiled diapers, **Sassy Diaper Sacks** ($3 for 50) are a nice alternative. Sized just right for a full diaper, their baby-powder scent goes a long way toward controlling odors. They're a good diaper-bag staple.

"For less-messy application of diaper rash cream, I squeeze it out onto the diaper instead of my baby's bottom."

▼ A CREAM, LIKE PALMER'S BOTTOM BUTTER, CAN BE A GENTLE SOOTHER ($4).

PALMER'S
COCOA BUTTER
FORMULA®

BOTTOM BUTTER

with
Pure Cocoa Butter
Vitamins A, D
& Pro Vitamin B5

Daily Soothing

SMOOTH APPLICATION

HELPS PREVENT, SOOTHE & TREAT DIAPER RASH

CLINICALLY AND
DERMATOLOGICALLY TESTED

NET WT. 125g/4.4 oz. ℮

106

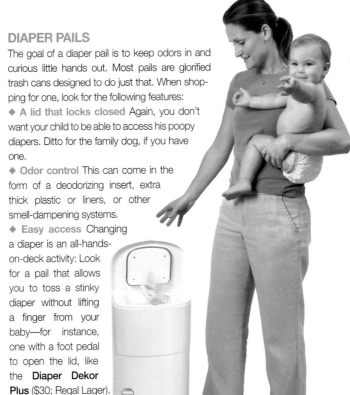

DIAPER PAILS

The goal of a diaper pail is to keep odors in and curious little hands out. Most pails are glorified trash cans designed to do just that. When shopping for one, look for the following features:

◆ **A lid that locks closed** Again, you don't want your child to be able to access his poopy diapers. Ditto for the family dog, if you have one.

◆ **Odor control** This can come in the form of a deodorizing insert, extra thick plastic or liners, or other smell-dampening systems.

◆ **Easy access** Changing a diaper is an all-hands-on-deck activity: Look for a pail that allows you to toss a stinky diaper without lifting a finger from your baby—for instance, one with a foot pedal to open the lid, like the **Diaper Dekor Plus** ($30; Regal Lager).

$KIP, $AVE, OR $PLURGE?

The **Diaper Genie** ($25; Playtex) is a diaper disposal system that uses a special plastic liner that twists each disposed-of diaper into its own section, so that you wind up with what looks like an oversized sausage link, with one diaper per link, to throw away. It was one of the most-mentioned products by our survey respondents. "It's amazing," raved one mom, "I'm a squeamish person and I had no problem with diapers and the smell." "It was a waste," groused another. If you have a friend who has one, go ahead and check it out before buying your own: Get her to show you how it works (and discreetly take a big sniff when you walk into her baby's room!). And keep in mind that you do have to buy replacement liners (about $6 per packet—enough for around 180 diapers), making this an ongoing cost commitment. On the other hand, if you don't think you'll have time to run out to the garbage can after every two or three diaper changes, the Genie can be a wish come true.

MOST KIDS AREN'T READY to potty train until they're at least 2½, and many wait even longer. (Don't believe what you read about infants learning to use the toilet; any triumphs belong to these babies' beleaguered *parents,* who are spending more time holding their bare-bottomed kids over the toilet than playing with them.) Don't push it; wait until your child shows these signs of being interested and ready. She will:

◆ watch you intently in the bathroom;
◆ seem to be bothered when she's wet or soiled;
◆ pull at her diaper;
◆ have words for pee and poop;
◆ seem to know when she's going or needs to go.

When she does, bring home a potty seat, put it in the bathroom, and just leave it there for a week or two. Let her look at it, play with it, put things inside it, and yes, if she wants to, sit on it (with her diaper on or off—her choice). Here are the features to look for in a potty seat:

◆ **Comfort** Buy a seat that your child will be able to sit on for prolonged periods. A simple "pot" of molded plastic, like the **Baby Bjorn Little Potty** ($10; babybjorn), might be more comfortable than a more complicated one with lots of bells and whistles. Let your child try several at the store; you may be able to tell which she prefers by watching her reaction to each.

◆ **Easy-to-clean** A separate "bowl" that can be removed and emptied into the big toilet is ideal.

◆ **A splash-guard** This is a little lip at the front of the seat that will block your child's urine from spraying on the floor.

◆ **Toilet paper holder** You might find this handy if you plan to set up the potty somewhere other than the bathroom. **My First Potty** ($15; Visionaire), a chunky little potty seat on four short legs that a child can straddle, has one.

▶ MY FIRST POTTY BY VISION-AIRE ($15) HAS A REMOVABLE LINER FOR EASY CLEANING AND DISPOSAL.

▶ BOON'S POTTY BENCH ($30) HAS SIDE POCKETS FOR BOOKS AND OTHER POTTY-TRAINING SUPPLIES.

◆ **A lid** Not absolutely necessary, but if you think that you'll have to let the spoils of a successful potty trip sit while you tend to other things (and especially if you have a dog!), a lid's not a bad idea. Plus, it will make your child's potty look more like the big one, and that can be a great incentive.

◆ **Handles** For carrying it room to room.

◆ **A kid-friendly design** Speaking of incentive, while you might prefer the tasteful, plain white potty that will blend in with your bathroom décor, chances are your child will want the one plastered with images of a favorite character, that also talks, plays music, and makes flushing noises. If that's what will make her want to use it, suck it up.

◆ **A seat that converts to a step stool** This is a good choice if you like the idea of getting the most bang for your buck. Plus, having one product do double duty will save space in a small bathroom. One of our favorites, the **Potty Bench** ($30; Boon), not only transforms into a

Mom Tip!

"To get my toddler to make regular tries on the potty, I put a sticker chart and stickers right beside it, so that she could get her reward right away."

sturdy stool when closed, it has two enclosed compartments (perfect for stashing books), a pull-out bowl, and a toilet paper holder.

◆ **A seat that turns the big toilet into one your toddler can use** Some kids want to go potty just like Mom and Dad. A well-padded insert for the regular toilet will be comfy for your child to sit on, and will make the opening in the toilet smaller so she doesn't tumble in. Many of these feature cute kid designs, like favorite cartoon characters. We love the **Ducka Potty Training Seat**, which is so lightweight your child can put it in place and hang it up when she's done ($20, Primo). You can also buy an insert that attaches with screws to a standard toilet so that it's always in place, like the **Flip 'n' Flush Training Seat** ($13; onestepahead.com), which comes in several colors. Grown-ups can flip it up and out of the way. Little ones will need a stool to get on and off of the big seat (with your help).

◀ FLIP 'N' FLUSH POTTY SEATS ($13) ALSO COME IN BRIGHT COLORS.

▶ LIGHT ENOUGH FOR LITTLE FINGERS: THE DUCKA POTTY TRAINING SEAT ($20) HAS NON-SLIP EDGING TO HOLD IT IN PLACE ON THE TOILET SEAT.

Mom Tip!

"I kept a jar of M&Ms in the bathroom so the reward for a successful trip to the potty was visible and handy."

Mom Tip!

"When I thought my son was ready to use the potty, we made a special trip to pick out big-boy superhero underpants."

POTTY TRAINING BOOKS One way to help a child achieve potty success is to read about it together. Some potty training books your toddler may enjoy (all available at amazon.com, Barnes & Noble, and, most likely, your public library):

◆ **What to Expect When You Use The Potty** by Heidi Murkoff and Laura Rader ($25; What to Expect Kids, HarperFestival). This book, co-authored by a *Parenting* contributing editor and the author of the popular *What to Expect* series on pregnancy and child-rearing, features a Scottish terrier named Angus who walks kids through the basics of toilet learning.

◆ **Once Upon a Potty** by Alona Frankel ($6; Firefly Books). A simple tale about a little girl who receives a potty from her grandmother, and having tried very hard, learns to use it—every time. Comes in a version for boys as well.

◆ **Sesame Beginnings: Potty Time** by Parker K. Sawyer ($6; Random House). The story features tod-dler Grover and his pals as they start to learn about potty training; there's a potty to "flush" at the end.

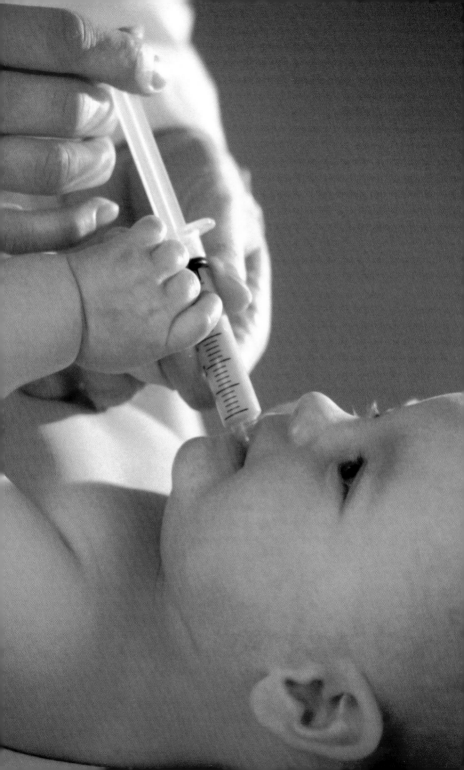

6

HEALTHY BABY

THE FIRST FEVER... the first case of sniffles… the first scraped knee…. These are the childhood milestones moms would love to skip—but most are as inevitable as a baby's first step. Our advice: Take a deep breath and accept that your child is going to get an upset tummy or drippy nose once in a while (and when he does, it won't be your fault!). Then make sure you have the following on hand to keep him from getting more than his fair share of illnesses and help him (and you!) feel better as soon as possible when he does get sick.

▲ RECTAL THER-
MOMETERS, LIKE
THIS ONE FROM
TIMEX ($16), ARE
THE MOST
ACCURATE WAY
TO TELL AN
INFANT'S
TEMPERATURE.

THERMOMETERS

It's important to have a thermometer that's both accurate and easy to use, especially in the first three months, when even a slight fever can be serious. The choices:

RECTAL Since a newborn's temperature is a key clue to his health, you'll want to be as exact as possible when taking it. The most reliable thermometer is a rectal one. As sticking one in your infant's bottom isn't so pleasant for either of you, opt for a digital model that registers quickly and is fail-safe, like **Vicks Baby Thermometer** ($13). The just-long-enough tip guarantees that you won't insert it too far. The **Timex Acrobat Bendable Thermometer with Indiglo** ($16) has a glow-in-the-dark face for nighttime readings, and it can take rectal and oral readings.

▶ THE FIRST
YEARS AMERICAN
RED CROSS
UNDERARM
THERMOMETER
($10) CAN
REGISTER
A TEMPERATURE
IN 8 SECONDS.

UNDERARM Compared to rectal ones, these are not as precise (they tend to register a degree low), but underarm thermometers, like the **First Years American Red Cross Underarm Thermometer** ($10; thefirstyears.com) may be better tolerated by older babies.

▶ IF YOU PREFER TO USE AN EAR THERMOMETER AT HOME, THE SUMMER INFANT ONE-SECOND EAR THERMOMETER ($30) IS AN EASY ONE TO USE.

Mom Tip!

"When taking my toddler's temperature under his arm, I just slip one arm out of the sleeve and tuck the thermometer under his shirt, He's more co-operative than if I took his shirt off altogether. "

EAR While it may look super-easy when the pediatrician does it, taking a child's temperature via his ear can be tricky, especially for babies under a year old: You have to aim the probe perfectly at the eardrum (not so easy when a kid is squirmy), and readings tend to be inconsistent.

PACIFIER If your baby loves binkies, you could try a pacifier thermometer. Keep in mind, though, that most pacifier models are half a degree low on average, so they're not the most accurate.

▶ THE LUMISCOPE BABYTHERM PACIFIER THERMOMETER ($15) BEEPS WHEN IT HAS REGISTERED A TEMPERATURE.

GIZMOS & GADGETS

Forehead thermometers that stick to a child's skin may be super-handy, but they're not very accurate. Avoid them altogether for babies, and if you use one on an older child, be aware that they're pretty good at detecting high fevers—but may miss a mild one. Use an oral thermometer after your child's fourth birthday.

115

◄ THE CRANE FROG HUMIDIFIER ($30) SHUTS OFF AUTOMATICALLY WHEN THE TANK IS EMPTY.

VAPORIZERS AND HUMIDIFIERS

The biggest difference between the two is that one moisturizes the air with warm steam and the other with a cool mist. Both have pros and cons, so talk to your pediatrician and consider the following before you buy:

◆ **Effectiveness** When breathed in, the steam emitted by a vaporizer, sometimes called a "warm mist humidifier," is better at loosening mucus and relieving a stuffy nose than the mist of a humidifier. Both do a fine job of returning moisture to the air to help relieve winter-dry skin. One humidifier that's particularly kid-friendly is the **Crane Frog 1-Gallon Humidifier** ($30). Not only is it cute, it's quiet, can accommodate rooms up to 500 square feet, and shuts off automatically when the tank is empty. It also comes in penguin, cow, panda, elephant, and dog shapes.

◆ **Safety** Because they don't get hot, humidifiers are safer than vaporizers, which pose a burn hazard. If you use one of the latter, keep it out of your baby's reach and never leave an older child alone with it.

◆ **Cleanliness** Because it heats the water, a vaporizer kills bacteria so that the steam is virtually germ-free. That said, **Sunbeam's PureMist Humidifier with UV Technology** ($40) automatically cleans germs right inside the unit.

▼ YOU CAN DO IT IN THE DARK: THE SUNBEAM PUREMIST HUMIDIFIER ($40) HAS A LIGHT INSIDE THE TANK SO YOU DON'T HAVE TO TURN ON LIGHTS TO CHECK THE WATER LEVEL.

▼ THE HELLO KITTY HUMIDIFIER ($40; CRANE) LETS YOU DECIDE HOW MUCH MOISTURE YOU WANT IT TO RELEASE.

◆ **Capacity** Be sure to choose a humidifier or vaporizer that's big enough for the room it will be used in. Read the label to check. Also make sure that it will hold enough water to last throughout the night; again, the label will tell you how frequently you'll need to refill the tank.

◆ **Upkeep** Both items require frequent changes of water to prevent buildup of bacteria.

◆ **Ease of use** Look for a vaporizer or humidifier that's easy to empty, fill, and clean (according to the manufacturer's instructions).

ULTRASONIC HUMIDIFIERS These use high-frequency sound waves to break water particles into a mist. **Crane** makes a **Hello Kitty** ultrasonic version ($40); **Sunbeam** makes one shaped like an aquarium ($50).

MEDICINE DROPPERS

Giving children liquid medicine is rarely easy, and when your baby doesn't feel well, it's only more difficult. There are number of gadgets available that will make the process more comfortable for both of you.

While most over-the-counter liquid pain relievers come with easy-to-use droppers, quite often prescription meds don't. It's a good idea to have an oral syringe on hand: It'll let you get the precise amount of drug out of the bottle and into your baby. Try the **EZ-Dose Oral Syringe 2 Teaspoon** ($3).

For particularly squirmy babies, the medicine nurser or pacifier syringe nurser, both from **EZ-Dose**, make medicating much simpler for babies who like to suck.

▲ THE EZ-DOSE MEDICINE NURSERS (ABOUT $3) ARE AN IDEAL SOLUTION FOR MEDICATING BABIES WHO LIKE THEIR BINKIES.

▲ HANDY TOOLS TO HELP THE MEDICINE GO DOWN: THE EZ-DOSE SYRINGE AND TEASPOON (ABOUT $3).

GIZMOS & GADGETS

A nasal aspirator, also called a bulb syringe, allows you to suck out the mucus that your child isn't able to blow out himself. A few drops of a saline solution in each nostril loosens the mucus so that it can be slurped out by the aspirator more easily. Hold your baby upright while you spray the saline and suction so he doesn't get a salty backdrip.

WHAT YOU NEED to help your baby feel better, no matter what ails him:

PAIN AND FEVER RELIEVERS Your choices are acetaminophen (Tylenol) and ibuprofen (Motrin or Advil). You might want to lay in some of both, as each have pros and cons:

Acetaminophen is gentler on the stomach and can be given to newborns, but it only lasts about 4 hours. **Ibuprofen** lasts for 6 to 8 hours (meaning you and your baby might get a decent night's sleep if given right before bedtime) and may be a more effective fever-reducer, but is only approved for babies 6 months and older. It's fine to use generic brands of both, as long as they're

labeled for infants or children. Some other things to consider when you're perusing pain-relievers for your child:

◆ **Method of delivery** Liquids are easiest to give most children (and your only option for babies and very little kids). Skip chewables and "meltables" until your child is older.

◆ **Flavor** Kids' meds are sweet and most will go down easily. Some kids prefer grape flavor over bubblegum. Go with what works.

◆ **Color** Some liquid medications, are clear, so that drips and spills won't stain. Try **Tylenol Dye-Free Cherry Flavor Infant Drops** ($9) or **Infants' Advil Concentrated Drops** ($4).

GAS RELIEVERS All babies are flatulence-prone, but if yours is clearly uncomfortable, with your doctor's OK

you might try a product like **Mylicon Infants' Gas Relief Drops** ($14), or gripe water (an infusion of dill, fennel, or caraway that has antispasmodic properties and may relax a baby's stomach and intestinal tract). You can find gripe water online or at many stores where you buy vitamins. One brand: **Little Tummys** ($9).

"To help soothe
my teething
7-month-old,
I gently place
an electric
toothbrush on
his gums (on a
low setting); the
vibration calms
him down."

TEETHING-PAIN RELIEVERS These are topical medicines designed to be rubbed directly on red, achy gums to numb and soothe them. One that's especially easy to use: **Baby Orajel Teething Swabs** ($6 for 12 swabs), which feature a handy applicator for dispensing the medicine. Another to look for: **Anbesol** ($6).

SALINE DROPS Use them to relieve a dry or stuffy nose: They're especially good for helping to break up mucus before you tackle it with a nasal aspirator. **Little Noses Saline Spray/Drops** ($3.50) can be used as both drops for a baby and a spray for an older child.

Mom Tip!

"I've discovered that most websites for particular drugstore products, like Tylenol or Orajel, offer printable coupons— usually for at least a dollar

REHYDRATING SOLUTION. These are drinks that can help to replace fluids in a child who's been vomiting or had severe diarrhea. The most popular, **Pedialyte,** comes in liters, single-serving sizes, and freezer pops; it's available in several different kid-friendly flavors, as well as unflavored (for infants), and is readily available in drugstores and supermarkets ($6 for four 8-ounce bottles, one 1-liter bottle, or 16 freezer pops).

WHAT NOT TO BUY
BYPASS THESE when stocking your child's medicine chest:

◆ **Aspirin** Never give a child of any age aspirin; it's been linked to a serious brain and liver disease called Reye's syndrome.

◆ **Decongestants, cough medicines, and other symptom-specific products** Even if they're labeled for babies, you should not use them for kids under 2 without the green light from your pediatrician. Ditto multisymptom products (such as cough-and-cold relievers): there's no need to give a child medicine to treat a cough, say, when she's not coughing.

◆ **Phenylpropanolamine** This ingredient has been found to trigger strokes and seizures; avoid any medicine that contains it.

Also, don't combine pain relievers without your doctor's OK, and be sure to use the formulation of medicine that's right for your child's age: Infant meds are more concentrated than kids' drugs, so an older child could easily overdose on a baby formulation.

119

7
BABY HANGOUTS

WHERE DO I PUT THE BABY?! Moms from many cultures deal with this question by simply strapping their kids onto their backs and going about their day. Our modern lifestyle rarely allows for such a simple solution. Fortunately, finding a parking spot for a baby—one that will keep her comfortable and cozy when she's sleepy, happy and entertained when she's awake, and safe and close by at all times—isn't a huge challenge, as long as you know what to look for. (There are so many seating options alone that we had to devote an entire chapter to them!) Here's a rundown of moms' favorite pointers and products to help you find the best arrangements for your baby (you'll probably want a few).

BOUNCY SEATS

THESE ARE LIKE LITTLE HAMMOCKS for babies, and they're a beautiful thing for the first few months. Just ask the moms in our survey, who considered their bouncy chair a "godsend" and the one thing they "couldn't live without."

Their reasons for loving this must-have:

◆ **Bouncy chairs are calming.** "I couldn't have survived the first few month without the bouncy seat. My daughter was very colicky and it's the only place she would sleep for the first six weeks."

◆ **Bouncy seats allow for mom time.** "She loved it, and then I could get some cleaning done or get in a shower."

◆ **They allow for together time.** "My baby especially liked the bouncy seat because she could sit close by and watch me."

◆ **They're fun.** "My son would kick his feet to activate the music and lights, or we would take the toy bar off and he'd nod off in the seat—it was the best purchase we made!"

◆ **Bouncy seats are versatile.** "As an infant, my son slept in it when we were downstairs. As he got older, it was a great place to seat him for feedings."

◆ **They're a safe hang-out.** "I was able to keep my kids where they could see what was going on without getting trampled."

◀ FISHER-PRICE MODELS, LIKE THE RAINFOREST BOUNCER ($40), GOT REPEATED RAVES IN OUR MOM SURVEY.

◀ ALTHOUGH YOUR HOME WILL INEVITABLY WIND UP LOOKING LIKE ROMPER ROOM, SOME BABY GEAR, LIKE OEUF'S BABY LOUNGER ($99), HAVE A DECIDEDLY SOPHISTICATED EDGE.

When shopping for a bouncy seat, make sure that it:

◆ **Is sturdy and stable.** The frame should be made of good-quality steel or aluminum, and it should sit firmly on a surface. It shouldn't be able to tip over no matter how vigorously it's bounced. (**NOTE:** Regardless of how stable a seat seems, you should never put your baby on a table top unless you're sitting right next to it, and never leave your baby alone in a bouncer.)

◆ **Is comfortable.** The fabric should cover and pad the hardware completely where it's within a baby's reach.

◆ **Is pinch-proof.** Check to see that there are no moving parts or other areas where curious fingers could get caught.

◆ **Has a seatbelt.** A 3- or-5 point restraining system is safest.

◆ **Provides head support.** If you plan to put your newborn in a bouncer, look for one that includes a headrest (permanent or removable) to cradle his head and neck.

◆ **Is easy to clean.** Make sure the fabric cover can be removed and tossed in the laundry.

Mom Tip!

(for multiples)
"As a mom of twins, I needed things that didn't take up a lot of room and could multi-task. The bouncy seat was great to feed them."

123

GIZMOS & GADGETS

The **Bumbo Baby Seat** is a one-piece contraption of molded, low-density foam that provides leg and back support for a baby who can't yet sit up on her own. Some of the moms in our survey really love theirs, while others felt the seats had a short lifespan, or their kids simply didn't like being in them. See if you can try one out at a friend's house before you buy ($40; six solid colors). The **Prince Lionheart BebePod** is another one-piece seating aid—this one in molded plastic—that warranted positive mentions in our survey. It's also about $40.

◆ **Will accommodate your baby for a reasonable amount of time.** Most seats are labeled according to how much weight they can take. (Some say they'll work for babies up to 40 pounds!) While you may be tempted to buy the seat that can hold the heaviest kid, keep in mind that once your baby is crawling, she won't want to be strapped into a bouncy seat.

◆ **Doesn't weigh a ton.** You'll probably be relocating it a lot. In fact, portability—being able to move the baby from room to room—is a must for many moms.

BEYOND THE BASICS It's hard to find a bouncer that just bounces; here are some of the optional features you'll find. Which you choose will depend on your goals for the seat (as simply a place for your baby to hang, snooze, and observe, or as a stimulating play experience), your price range, and your aesthetics.

◆ **A vibrating function** This was the bouncy chair feature our surveyed moms praised the most. "The vibrating bouncy seat is the best thing ever invented for babies!" Moms especially loved several of the models made by **Fisher-Price,** including the **Baby Papasan Infant Seat** ($50) and the **Ocean Wonders Aquarium Bouncer** ($40). (Fisher-Price makes ten different bouncers.)

◆ **Canopy** This will make the space cozy for sleeping. Look for one that's removable, or that you can fold back out of the way, once your baby is older.

◆ **Adjustable seat** A bouncer that can recline for an infant, then be adjusted to a more upright position for an older baby, will allow you to get more use out it. For example, **Summer's Infant Deluxe Soft Embrace Bouncer** ($50) has a 3-position reclining seat.

◆ **A toy bar** Typically this is an arc that fits over the chair, which puts hanging playthings within easy reach. Look for a toy bar that's removable, and for toys that can be removed, too, so that you can exchange them for other items when your baby gets bored.

◆ **Music and lights** It might be a melody that plays when you flick a switch, or it might make sounds in response to your baby's kicking and grasping. The **LeapFrog Magic Moments Learning Seat** repays kicking feet and curious hands with tunes, rhymes, or twinkling lights ($50).

Mom Tip!

"I wanted a plain seat that wouldn't require batteries. When I couldn't find one, I simply never put the batteries in the seat I finally purchased. My baby didn't know the difference—he loved his bouncer anyway."

124

◆ **Versatility** Some bouncers also rock; the **Fisher-Price Infant Seat to Toddler Rocker** does just what it says—converts to a rocking chair for older babies and tots ($33).

◆ **Folds for storage or travel** Graco's **Travel Bouncer** gets extra points for having a carry bag ($50), while **Infantino's On-the-Go Lounger** is a bargain at just $20.

◆ **A remote** We know of only one bouncer that has one, but for a weary mom, it can be a nice perk: The **Summer Infant Remote Control Seat** lets you activate the bouncing or vibrating modes from across the room ($40).

◆ **Sophisticated design** Not every mom wants her baby's bouncy seat to sport a lot of bells and whistles. Ironically, you'll pay more for such simplicity. For instance, the **Bouncing Baby Lounger** by **Oeuf** ($99) is as sleek and modern as they come: It just sits there looking cool (it comes in chocolate brown with a simple, wide pink or blue stripe) and bounces gently in response to a baby's movements.

▲ TO GET MORE BANG FOR YOUR BUCK, LOOK FOR PRODUCTS THAT "GROW" WITH YOUR BABY, LIKE THIS INFANT SEAT THAT BECOMES A ROCKER FROM FISHER-PRICE ($33).

PLAY MATS & GYMS

AT ITS MOST BASIC, a play mat is a padded mat with a bar that arcs over it from which toys hang, to entertain a baby who's lying on her back. The mat itself is usually colorful and fun to look at as well, for when a baby's on her stomach and able to push up with her arms. Most play mats are that and more. The same goes for gyms, which are bars with toys (with or without a mat underneath).

A good mat (or gym) is not hard to find. There are options to suit your price range, your baby's needs, and your own preferences. Here are the things to look for, as well as the optional features you might want in both a mat and a gym (keep in mind that the two are pretty redundant—most families don't need both):

◆ **Ample padding** Chances are you'll spread the mat out on top of a rug or carpet, but since your baby will be lying on it you'll want it to be as comfy as possible. A mat that's quilted is ideal.

◆ **Easy to clean** Make sure the mat is labeled "machine washable."

◆ **Easy setup and take-down** Some mats require you to remove the toy bar each time you fold up the mat, and reassemble it again for play time. Others can be folded up and stored intact, like the **Fisher Price Miracles & Milestones Pop Open Play Mat** ($40).

◆ **Interchangeable toys** The toys that come with the mat should be removable, and there should be hooks or links that allow you to hang other playthings from it. **Tiny Love**, for example, sells extra toys for its mats, like the **Gymini 3-D Activity Gym** ($40), one of our surveyed mom's favorites: "Great portability, great entertainment—and the toys hang low enough for batting practice." So does **Lamaze**. Its **Link Along Friends** are about $20 for a set of three plush toys.

◆ **Noise makers** Look for squeakers, crinklers, rattles, and jingles—not just among the toys, but also on the mat itself. Some have soundmakers built right in.

◄ SPACE SAVER: PORTABLE PLAY-MATS, LIKE THIS FISHER-PRICE POP-OPEN PLAYMAT ($40), ARE A GOOD SOLUTION FOR SMALL ROOMS.

▶ PLAY MATS WITH TWO TOY BARS, LIKE THIS GYMINI TOTAL PLAYGROUND ($70), MEANS THAT ARMS AND LEGS CAN GET A GOOD WORKOUT-WHATEVER YOUR BABY'S POSITION.

◆ **Lights and music** Some mats have features that light up or play music when played with. Try these out in the store to make sure the sound quality is good enough (meaning, it won't drive you crazy). And of course, a mat like this will require batteries. We like the **Baby Einstein Discover & Play Activity Gym** ($60) for its ten dangling toys and music by Bach and Beethoven.

◆ **Designed for tummy time** Because babies sleep on their backs and spend much of their waking time in that position as well, it's important to place them on their bellies for short periods of supervised time during the day. This gives them the chance to strengthen the muscles that allow them to raise their upper bodies off the ground—a first step toward crawling. Many have detachable pillows that are designed for propping up a belly-side-down baby—like the **Tummy Time Prop & Play Mat** ($40) or **Infantino's Surfboard Tummy Time Mat** ($20). Note that most tummy-time specific mats are meant for babies 3 months and up. The pillows could pose a suffocation risk for newborns.

◆ **Foot action** Gyms that keep tiny tootsies busy can be especially fun (and help teach about cause-and-effect). **Chicco's Duo Play Gym** ($40), for example, has foot pedals that respond to being pressed or kicked with lights, sounds, and music.

◀ THE ACTIVITY PANEL ON THE CHICCO DUO PLAY GYM ($40) CAN ALSO BE ATTACHED TO THE SIDE OF YOUR BABY'S CRIB.

127

SWINGS

MOM-TESTED! SURVEY

50% of the moms in our survey said that a swing helped them get their babies to sleep more than any other item.

BABIES LOVE SWINGS: The back-and-forth motion reminds them of being swayed in the womb, and is soothing and satisfying, especially for a cranky baby. Moms are fans too: "I absolutely love the baby swing. When I can't console my baby, the swinging and music calm her down right away," said one satisfied mom-tester. Said another, "The swing got my baby to sleep when nothing else would work." Other moms in our survey noted that they could plop their baby in the swing for long enough to take a quick shower or throw in a load of laundry: "It gave me peace of mind to pump, or shower, especially because I'm a single mom and don't have an extra set of hands."

The downside to swings? They can be so effective that it can become all too easy to leave a baby in it for long periods of time. But babies need to experience a variety of environments throughout the day, and a swing or other contraption should never replace one-on-one time with mom or dad. Some experts also advise not putting a baby to sleep in a swing; she can become dependent on it. We say it's probably okay once in a while: How else will you get your own shut-eye?

Mom Tip!

"When I was swing shopping online, I discovered an awesome feature at fisher-price.com: an at-a-glance chart that compares all the company's swings according to features. It made choosing a swing a snap. The site also has comparison charts for their high chairs and bouncers."

Most swings are designed to hold babies up to 25 pounds. Expect to pay from around $50 to $140 for a good-quality, name-brand swing. Here are some mom-tested features and product recommendations to bear in mind as you shop:

◆ **Sturdy construction** The frame of the swing should be of good-quality steel or other metal and be designed to sit squarely on the floor; it shouldn't be able to tip at all. The swing should be securely attached to the frame. (If you assemble the swing yourself, make sure that you follow directions to the letter and that every bolt and screw is in place and tight.)

◆ **Nonskid base** The swing should stay in place while in motion.

◆ **Smooth movement** Make sure it moves fluidly and doesn't jerk, and that it doesn't move too quickly.

◆ **Adjustable speed** Some swings have as many as eight speeds, making it easy to find one that your baby likes best.

GIZMOS & GADGETS

If your child is at least 4 months old and can sit unassisted, you might invest in a jumper—a harness that hangs from a doorway and allows your baby to use his feet to bounce. The classic **Johnny Jump Up** ($20) can be used for non-walkers up to 24 pounds. An alternative is a freestanding jumper. Lots of moms in our survey cited the **Fisher-Price Deluxe Jumperoo** (right, $70) as one of their best-loved baby items.

◆ **Quiet action** Pass on any swing that's creaky or has a loud motor.

◆ **A comfy, washable seat pad** It should provide ample support, especially for a newborn who hasn't yet developed control of her head and neck.

◆ **A reclining seat** This feature is optional but useful; some swings can recline all the way back, and some also have several different reclining options to accommodate babies at different stages of development. A seat that can be adjusted with one hand is a plus.

◆ **Good head clearance** You should be able to get your baby in and out of the swing without bumping her head on the frame. An "open-top" swing is ideal because it's designed without an overhead bar.

◆ **Safety restraint** A 3- or 5-point safety belt is a must.

◆ **Side-to-side motion** Some swings can be set to move sideways as well as back and forth—a feature that came up as a plus over and over again in our mom survey. Two mom-tested swings by Fisher-Price were especially popular: the **Ocean Wonders Aquarium Cradle Swing** ($120) and the **Baby Papasan Cradle Swing** ($130).

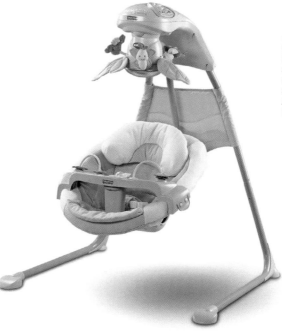

◄ THE FISHER-PRICE BABY PAPASAN CRADLE SWING SWINGS FROM SIDE TO SIDE AS WELL AS BACK AND FORTH.

130

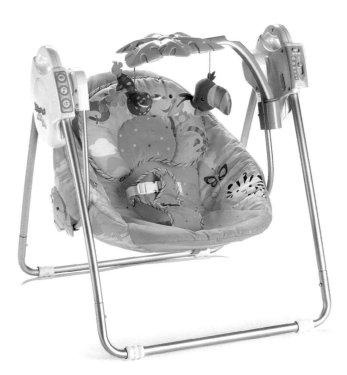

◆ **Entertainment** This can be as simple as a toy bar or tray (removable ones are best) or an overhead mobile, or as sophisticated as lights and music. The **Graco Silhouette Swing** ($120), for example, plays both classical music and nature sounds.

◆ **Easy storage and transport** "We love the **Fisher-Price Aquarium Take-Along Swing**," says a mom of twins. "We bought two, and they're great for getting the babies to take naps at Grandma's house" ($65). Many moms value portability in a swing and opted for travel-size models. Several moms in our survey mentioned that they liked being able to move their swing from room to room to keep the baby nearby. One especially appreciated that her portable swing "takes up very little room and folds up very easily to take to a friend's house."

◆ **Plug-in option** Run-down batteries were a sore point for the moms in our survey. That's why several were quick to praise the **Fisher-Price Power Plus Swing** ($85), which can be plugged in, eliminating the need for batteries altogether.

▲ FISHER-PRICE'S RAIN-FOREST OPEN TOP TAKE-ALONG SWING ($65) TRAVELS EASILY FROM ROOM TO ROOM—OR TO GRANDMA'S AND BACK.

YOUR MOM CALLED IT A PLAYPEN—a term that fell out of favor some years ago, given that it sounds like a jail for babies, rather than the safe place for hanging out that it really is. Strictly speaking, a play yard is a portable play space that's enclosed on all sides and has a soft, comfortable surface for a baby to sit or lie on. Nowadays, very few play yards take on this single role; most double as portable cribs and include accessories that transform them into bassinets, changing tables, and more. (See pages 156–157 for more about these multitalented products.)

Here we'll just talk about play yards designed simply as a spot to park a mobile baby with some toys when you need to do something else. **Graco, Evenflo,** and **Baby Trend** all sell basic play yards in the $40 to $100 range. They're usually a cheaper option than multifunctional play yards and portable cribs, so consider which you really need; it may be unnecessary to buy both.

▲ SOME PLAY YARDS LIKE THE PHIL & TED'S T2 TRAVEL COT FROM REGAL LAGER ($150) ARE DESIGNED FOR OUTDOOR USE, WITH WATERPROOF FABRIC AND UV SHADED MESH.

A FEW SAFETY NOTES: Don't stock a play yard with toys that a child could use to stand on and climb out. And if you receive a secondhand one, log on to cpsc.gov (the Consumer Products Safety Commission) to make sure it hasn't been recalled. More than 10 million play yards made before 1998 have been taken off the market because of faulty rails and protruding rivets.

What to look for in a simple play yard:
◆ mesh sides, so your baby can see out and you can see in
◆ a frame that locks securely in place
◆ a comfortable bottom
◆ washable surface (You should be able to wipe it down easily)
◆ lightweight construction (You'll want to be able to move it easily from room to room, so that your baby is always within sight.)
◆ easy to set up and break down
◆ a storage bag for travel
◆ optional entertainment (The **Graco Pack 'n' Play Playmat Combo** features a detachable gym; $100.)

◄ DOUBLE DUTY: THIS PLAY YARD FROM COMBI ($120) IS ALSO A CHANGING TABLE.

133

ACTIVITY CENTERS

THESE TYPICALLY CONSIST OF A PLASTIC TABLE with a cushioned seat in the middle that swivels all the way around. Most have toys attached and can be the perfect hangout for babies who are able to sit on their own and support most of their weight with their legs. They're a safe alternative to walkers, which are not recommended for any child, but shouldn't be overused. Kids need to be able to crawl around in order to build muscle strength and sharpen their large motor skills.

Most moms love 'em, though some babies might not be intrigued by all the attached toys. This would be a good product to try out at a friend's house before you buy. And if you do, expect to shell out from $45 to $80 for a stationary activity center. To make sure you get enough bang for your buck, a good activity center should:

◆ **be sturdy as a rock.** By design (wider at the bottom than at the top), they're virtually untippable anyway.

▶ A STANDARD, (AND A MOM-TESTED FAVORITE), THE EVENFLO EXERSAUCER COMES IN SEVERAL VERSIONS WITH DIFFERENT FEATURES AND AT DIFFERENT PRICES ($60 TO $120).

134

◆ **have smooth working parts.** If it rotates 360 degrees, it should spin easily. For example, if it bounces, your child should be able to move it up and down without straining.

◆ **fit your child.** A baby in a stationary play center should be able to touch both feet to the floor (or the bottom of the play center), with her waist at or below table level. (Once she can walk, grows taller than 32 inches, or weighs 30 pounds, it's time to put the center away.)

◆ **include stimulating, entertaining toys.** These can be as simple as balls that spin in place to electronic toys like the ones featured on the **Baby Einstein Music & Motion Activity Jumper** ($80); it has light-up piano keys that play five classical melodies, among several other developmental activities.

▲ NEVER A DULL MOMENT: THIS BABY EINSTEIN JUMPER HAS TOYS GALORE ($80).

◆ **do double duty.** This is optional, but a can be a plus. Some activity centers convert to other toys once a child outgrows them. For example, the **Baby Sit & Step 2-in-1 Activity Center** ($80) turns into a walk-behind walker (your baby can push it). **Baby Trend's Bouncer and Entertainment Table** ($30) converts to a play table.

◆ **be easy to move around.** It should be, at least, if you think you'll want to move it around to different rooms. The **Exersaucer Ultra 2 in 1** ($80; Evenflo) folds up and features a built-in handle.

$KIP, $AVE, OR $PLURGE?

Seating options for pre-walkers have a limited lifespan: Each hangout—from bouncy seat to Exersaucer—will only serve your baby for a few months. So should you always buy these items new? Not necessarily: You can often find used baby seating in tip-top condition at yard sales and consignment stores. Often these items are like the used car Grandma only drove to church on Sundays: in pristine condition. Evaluate a "pre-owned" item just as you would a new one. Make sure it:

◆ looks and feels sturdy.

◆ has no broken parts or dysfunctional features (the seat on a play center doesn't spin smoothly, a bouncy seat's canopy won't stay up).

◆ has no small pieces that have come off or seem about to come off.

◆ hasn't been recalled (check if you can).

◆ looks clean (or at least cleanable).

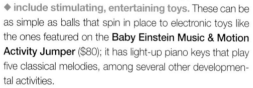

8 ON THE GO

FOR SOME NEW MOMS, the biggest achievement after bringing a baby into the world is taking him right back out again—that is, getting out of the house with a newborn and all his requisite gear. For more seasoned moms, the biggest achievement of any given day may well be the same thing; bringing a baby or toddler along on any errand, no matter how large or small, can be a challenge.

As important as what you carry your baby's stuff in is what you carry him in. Besides pushing him in a stroller, you may want to "wear" him—in a carrier or backpack. And, of course, you'll need a car seat, which—more than any other item—needs to be purchased with care.

There are myriad products to help make baby-schlepping as easy as possible—starting with a well-stocked diaper bag. No matter how sleek or fancy your bag is, it won't be worth beans if it's filled with the wrong stuff. Use this list of essentials to check that your bag has everything you need—and nothing more:

DON'T FORGET...

◆ **Diapers** Bring one more than you think you'll need, based on the amount of time you plan to be out and how frequently you change your baby.

◆ **Wipes** A slender, portable wipes case or a resealable plastic bag should hold plenty and won't take up too much space.

◆ **Nourishment** This can be a bottle (or two, if you'll be gone for more than a few hours) and formula (or jarred food or toddler snacks, depending on your baby's age). If you're nursing exclusively, just tuck in some nursing pads.

◆ **Burp cloth** This is important whether you're breast- or bottle feeding.

◆ **A change of clothes** For an infant, a one-piece footed outfit is easier to bring along than separates; for an older baby or toddler, bring an extra top (in case of spills) and bottom (in case of leaks). Slip these into a large resealable plastic bag, which you can then put the dirty duds in.

◆ **One favorite toy** Preferably your baby's lovey, if he has one.

◆ **Baby sunblock** This is a must for a baby over 6 months (if you live in a warm climate and/or if your baby will be in the sun).

◆ **Hand gel** or antibacterial hand wipes.

◆ **A water bottle** A small snack for you, such as a nutrition bar, is a good idea also—especially if you're nursing.

◆ **Stain remover** We like **Shout Wipes** ($3 for twelve) or **Tide-to-Go Pen** ($3 per pen).

◆ **Small pack of tissues**

◆ **Changing pad**

FORGET ABOUT...

extra toys, rattles, or books (your keys or an empty water bottle will entertain in a pinch); bibs (you can use the burp cloth); rash cream and other meds, unless your baby has a blazing red bottom or you expect to be out all day; receiving blankets.

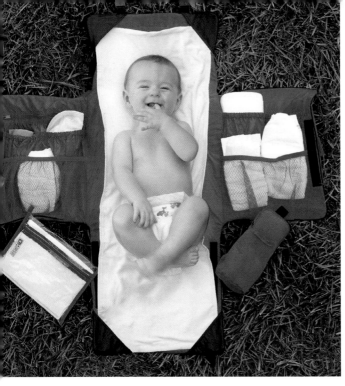

◄ IT'S ALL INSIDE:
THE BABY
TRAVELLER
(ABOUT $80;
REGAL LAGER)
HAS A POCKET
FOR EVERYTHING.

LIKE MATERNITY CLOTHES, diaper bags have evolved from dowdy and juvenile-looking necessities into fashionable yet practical accessories. Even Kate Spade, the hip, high-end purse designer, has a line of diaper bags. And while not many women can justify dropping a bundle on a bag, there are plenty of stylish options out there now for much less.

You can buy cool diaper bags anywhere you buy baby gear (stores like Baby Depot, Buy Buy Baby and Babies 'R' Us, megastores like Wal-Mart and Target, kids' clothing boutiques, online sites that sell baby products). And you can pay as little as $30 (such as for a Lands' End canvas diaper bag; landsend.com) to many times that.

◄ HIGH-END BAGS
LIKE KATE SPADE'S
FLATIRON HENRY
BABY BAG ($415)
CAN GO FROM THE
PLAYGROUND TO
THE OFFICE.

139

Whatever you spend, you'll want to look for convenient features like:

◆ **Lots of pouches** and slots inside and out (make sure at least one is large enough to hold a couple of diapers).

◆ **A roomy interior** that can accommodate a favorite toy and a change of clothes.

◆ **Insulated bottle holder** (it may not always be an option, but it's a nice touch).

◆ **Changing pad** Note that these are often little more than a scrap of coordinating fabric with a waterproof backing; you may want to consider buying a separate changing pad (see page 142).

◆ **Easy upkeep** The most practical bags are made of a washable or wipeable fabric inside and out, such as nylon or vinyl. Make sure the inside is waterproof: Spills are inevitable.

◆ **Weather resistance** (a must for any bag you plan to use out of doors—on long stroller walks, for example).

◆ **Easy to carry** Look for adjustable shoulder straps, for example, or backpacks, if you like that style. The **JJ Cole Logic Bag** ($30) is long and lean instead of wide and bulky, and can be slung across your back or clipped onto your stroller.

◆ **Unisex appeal** This is important if you want to make sure Dad shares in on-the-go diaper duty. For example, the messenger-bag style totes by **Diaper Dude** ($60) are plain or sport manly motifs (camouflage, peace signs) as well as plenty of pockets for wipes and other baby stuff.

▲ THE SIDEKICK BY PARENTS OF INVENTION ($80) CONVERTS TO A BABY CARRIER.

▲ THE JJ COLE LOGIC BAG ($30) IS IDEAL FOR MOMS (AND DADS) WHO PREFER A SLEEK SILHOUETTE.

◀ DIAPER DUDE BAGS ($60) ARE ALSO AVAILABLE IN A MINI SIZE THAT CAN BE WORN LIKE A FANNY PACK.

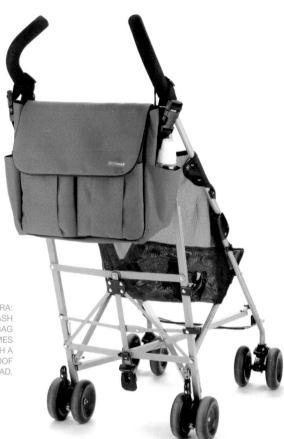

▶ A NICE EXTRA:
THE DASH
DIAPER BAG
($68) COMES
WITH A
WATERPROOF
CHANGING PAD.

GIZMOS & GADGETS

If changing your baby in public restrooms gives you the willies, you might bring along an extra layer of protection, like **PeeWees Disposable Multi-Use Pads** ($16 for a box of 36). Just toss after using.

▼ FLEURVILLE'S MOTHERSHIP BAG ($150) IS NOT ONLY GREAT-LOOKING, BUT THE WATER-PROOFING USED ON THE OUTSIDE IS ENVIRONMEN-TALLY FRIENDLY.

◆ **Stroller-friendliness** If you plan to be behind the wheels much of the time, look for a bag that's designed to hang from the stroller, like the **Dash diaper bag** by **Skip Hop** ($68; skiphop.com). Besides a removable shoulder strap, it features two loops on either side that slip easily over the handles of an umbrella stroller. (SkipHop also makes a bag that can be attached to the side of a standard stroller.)

◆ **Lightweight** You can fill it up without making it too heavy.

◆ **Attractiveness** One of our surveyed moms especially loves her **Fleurville Mothership** diaper bag: "It's fashionable, sturdy, easy to clean, and has lots of storage!" ($150).

141

◆ **Versatility** The Regal Lager **gr8x Baby Traveller Deluxe** ($80) gives you the best of both worlds, and more: Not only can it be configured as either a backpack or shoulder bag, it unfolds into a changing pad and comes with an insulated bottle holder.

Products to consider besides—or instead of—a conventional diaper bag:

◆ **A bottle bag** If you're bottle-feeding and need to keep breast milk, formula, or baby food fresh, you may want to purchase an insulated bottle carrier. Some require an ice pack; others can be chilled in the fridge or freezer, or feature an insulated lining that will keep cold liquids cold and warm liquids warm for several hours. Some bags will hold several bottles (including a water bottle or soda for you); you can also find bottle carriers with space for keys, cell phones, pacifiers—even diapers and wipes!

◆ **A changing pad** If the one that comes with your diaper bag is less than ideal (and most are), a separate surface for diaper duty can come in handy. (Yes, you can tuck a receiving blanket or burp cloth under your baby's bum, but if he's had a blowout poop, you won't be using that blanket or cloth for anything else while you're out!) An innovative option: Round changing pads that allow you to position your baby in any direction; if he squirms, no prob-

▲ WITH A LEAK-PROOF LINING, THE MULTI-PURPOSE MAXICOOL BOTTLE BAG FROM J.L. CHILDRESS (ABOUT $10) WILL MAKE SURE EVERY-THING ELSE IN YOUR DIAPER BAG IS PROTECTED.

lem—he'll still be centered on the pad. Designed by a mom, **Patemm changing pads** ($30 to $48, depending on size and whether the pad has pockets) come in pretty, stylish prints, and fold into a neat rectangle—with handles—that fits easily in most diaper bags. Some come with pockets large enough to tuck diapers and wipes into as well. One of the moms in our survey tipped us off to her favorite portable pad: the **First Years Deluxe Fold 'n' Go Diaper Kit,** which features pockets for diapers, supplies, keys, and money, but folds up into one small package—for just $8!

◆ **A diaper tote** For super-quick trips or once your child hits the toddler stage, you might consider a scaled-down carrier that holds just enough for one diaper change. While a resealable plastic bag will do just fine, we love the **Diaper Pack by 2redhens** ($22; 2redhens.com): These sturdy, pretty zippered bags are sized to perfectly fit one or two diapers plus a travel pack of wipes, zip at the top, and have a convenient strap for hanging on a stroller. For walks, check out **phil&teds Hang Bag** ($25; regallager.com), a scaled-down bag that'll hold just what your baby needs for a short outing. You can hang it from the stroller or wear it like a fanny pack.

◆ **An alternative to a bag for dads** Check out the fleece **DadGear Diaper Vest** ($82; dadgear.com), which has hidden pockets for bottles, wipes, a pacifier, and more.

143

BABY CARRIERS

BABIES LOVE TO BE CLOSE to you, and so a contraption that allows you to "wear" your baby will not only provide a convenient mode of conveyance when, for instance, a stroller is impractical, it'll allow you and your child to enjoy a special chance to bond. There are three main types of baby carrier; which you choose will depend on your baby's age and stage, as well as which you and your child prefer: Many babies have a definite preference for being toted in one position versus another, and no doubt yours will let you know if he doesn't like the carrier you put him in.

Moms are equally picky when it comes to carriers, a fact that came through loud and clear in our survey. So if you can, borrow a carrier to test with your baby, to avoid shelling out for one that doesn't suit. And once you buy one, give yourself some time to get used to it. One of the moms in our survey said of her Baby Bjorn carrier: "It's easy to use once you get the hang of it—that takes about three wearings."

▲ FOR NICER WALKS: THE BABY BJORN CARRIER ACTIVE ($120) OFFERS MORE BACK AND SHOULDER SUPPORT THAN THE ORIGINAL MODEL, SO YOU CAN CARRY YOUR BABY FOR LONGER PERIODS OF TIME.

SLINGS

At its simplest, a baby sling is practically primitive—little more than a swath of fabric that wraps around your body diagonally (over one shoulder to the opposite hip) to create a "hammock" for your baby to snuggle in. Most moms use them primarily for infants, although some slings can be configured to hold larger babies and even toddlers in an upright or hip-straddling position. Proponents of baby slings claim that they promote bonding since they allow for close, face-to-face contact. Some mothers are able to breast-feed while their baby's in a sling. Other fans just like them because they're relatively simple to use, and affordable (about $30 to $60). Several petite moms in our survey preferred slings to front carriers because they found them more comfortable.

Although chain stores—both baby-specific ones like Baby Depot and Babies 'R' Us and general ones like Target—offer a few baby slings in their stores and on their websites, these tend to be more elaborate slings by name-brand baby-gear makers. If you're interested in a truly simple fabric sling, try babyslings.com and amazon.com for basic models.

▼ A ZOLOWEAR
SLING ($79–$159)
ALLOWS YOU
TO CARRY YOUR
BABY A NUMBER
OF DIFFERENT
WAYS.

If possible, try on several slings (if you order from a website, make sure you can return a rejected sling easily) to see what feels most comfortable. Features to consider:

◆ **Adjustable shoulder strap** Classic slings have a double ring at one end, through which you weave the other end to adjust the sling to fit your body and to position your baby where it's most comfortable for you. Some parents like to wear their babies low, some high. This type of sling leaves a long piece of fabric just hanging; try one before buying to see if it bothers you. One of the moms in our survey loved her **Zolowear** sling; it runs from $79 for a basic cotton sling to $159 for one fashioned from silk brocade.

More elaborate slings may adjust with zippers or buckles. And some slings are just a wide swath of stretchy fabric; they're often described as "pouches."

145

▲ THE ULTIMATE BABY WRAP FROM PARENTS OF INVENTION ($46) FITS A BABY FROM BIRTH TO AGE 3.

◆ **Padded shoulder strap** It can make baby-wearing more comfortable.

◆ **Padding for the baby** This not only makes for a cushier ride, it also creates a more structured sling. The downside: A padded sling will be bulkier and not as easy to tuck into a diaper bag for transport.

◆ **Optional configurations** Some slings are designed so that you can use them in different ways. For instance, the **Nojo Original Baby Sling,** developed by *Parenting* contributing editor Dr. William Sears ($30), can be adjusted in four positions and used for a child up to 30 pounds. The **Ultimate Baby Wrap** carrier ($46) can be worn in five different positions (and is packaged with video directions and a carrying bag).

◆ **Washable fabric** A must. Spit-up—and more—happens, especially with very young babies.

◆ **Pockets and other storage features** The **Premaxx Baby-Bag** ($48; premaxx.com), for instance, has zippered compartments that can hold keys, cash, or a pacifier.

▲ YOU CAN ADJUST THE NOJO BABY SLING ($30) WITH ONE HAND.

Some of the brands moms our survey touted as their favorites:

◆ **Jelly Beans Baby Slings** These slings are handmade by a mom in Texas. They're reversible and washable (from $45, depending on size and fabric; jellybeansbabyslings.com).

◆ **Kangaroo Korner Adjustable Pouches** This sling-style carrier simply wraps around your body, with no hardware to adjust. "I love that it's so easy to 'wear' my baby. No snaps or buckles to fasten—just plop the baby in and go!" ($60; kangarookorner.com).

◆ **Maya Wrap slings** "It's adjustable so you can hold the baby in all different positions, and you can even use it as a hip or back carrier for a toddler" ($50 for an unpadded sling; $55 for a lightly padded sling; mayawrap.com). One mother described her Maya Wrap sling as "my third and fourth hands with both my boys. I don't know how I'd have survived their babyhood without it."

◆ **The Peanut Shell** Several moms mentioned this pouch-type sling, which comes in a ton of cool patterns ($48).

▲ THE PREMAXX BABY-BAG CARRIES YOUR NEWBORN IN A POSITION SIMILAR TO WHEN HE WAS IN THE WOMB ($48).

146

FRONT CARRIERS

More structured (and arguably more complicated) than a sling, a front carrier is a harness-like carrier that allows you to strap your baby to your chest in an upright position, facing either in or out. The most popular brands of front carriers are **Baby Bjorn**—"It was comfortable and got me through two children and still looked new!"—(these have many fans and run from $80 to $120, depending on the model) and **Snugli** ($20 to $30), but plenty of other options abound anywhere you can buy other baby products.

Features to consider when shopping for a front carrier:

◆ **Back-of-the-head support** Infants who can't support their head should face inward, and will need a sturdy means of support behind them. The back of the carrier should be of a firm material and extend at least as high as the baby's head.

◆ **Leg openings** They should be large enough so that your child can kick his legs freely, but snug enough so that he doesn't slump downward to one side.

◆ **Versatility** Most carriers fit infants up to 20 or 25 pounds and many allow older babies to face outward once they can hold their head up.

◆ **Sturdy construction** If you want your carrier to get you through both the inward- and outward-facing phase, choose one that's well made, like the **Baby Bjorn Carrier Active** ($120).

◆ **Back support—for you** You should be able to adjust the carrier so that your child's weight is distributed evenly:

▼ A DIAPER BAG AND BABY CARRIER IN ONE: THE PARENTS OF INVENTION SIDEKICK ($80).

The **Ergo Baby Carrier** ($92), which functions as both a front- and back-carrier, does this, and features a wide, padded waist belt for added comfort for you.

◆ **Storage** You don't want to weigh yourself down with a lot of extra stuff, but the bottle holder on the **Evenflo Snugli Serenade** ($60) can certainly come in handy. You might also consider the innovative two-in-one practicality of the **Parents of Invention Sidekick** ($80), which neatly converts from baby carrier to diaper bag.

◆ **For older babies and toddlers** Once your child makes the shift to straddling your hip, you might want to consider a carrier that will help take on some of his weight, like the **Hip Baby Carrier** ($92; Walking Rock Farm). A less pricey option is the **Hip Hammock** ($40; Playtex), which allows you to hold a baby between 15 and 35 pounds on either hip.

BACKPACKS

These typically consist of a steel frame covered in fabric to create a perch for an older baby (age 6 months and up) on mom's or dad's back. Because they're modeled after backpacks used for hiking, many sport lots of compartments for gear, making them especially multifunctional. Some are too heavy for everyday use, but several of the moms in our survey actually preferred a backpack carrier to a front carrier while doing household chores, because the latter got in the way of doing things like emptying the dishwasher. You can buy backpack carriers anywhere baby products are sold, as well as at outdoor stores and on websites that offer camping and outdoor gear. Two popular brands to check out: **Gerry** and **Kelty.** Note that with backpacks, you really need to try them on before purchasing—a good fit is essential.

▲ THE HIP BABY CARRIER ($92) IS SUITABLE FOR CHILDREN UP TO 45 POUNDS.

What to look for in a back pack carrier:

◆ **Sturdy construction** The frame shouldn't jiggle or feel loose. All screws and connections between parts should be tight.

◆ **Ample fabric** It should fully surround and support your child and cover up and soften any hard or sharp edges of the frame.

◆ **Lightweight,** so you're not lugging around extra weight.

◆ **Support for your child** The carrier should hold your baby comfortably upright and snugly against your body (without being too confining).

◆ **Well-proportioned leg openings** Your child should be able to kick his legs freely but with no danger of slipping through.

◆ **A 5-point safety belt** like those recommended for car seats, strollers, and other gear.

▶ PERFECT FOR HIKERS WHO WANT TO BRING THEIR CHILD ALONG: THE KELTY ADVENTURE FRAME BACKPACK ($240).

◆ **Fully adjustable, padded straps** Make sure the carrier is designed to fit your body: Some are better suited for taller or shorter people, so check the box for specifics. You should be able to adjust the carrier so that your baby's weight is distributed equally across your body and so that your lower back doesn't feel strained.

◆ **Extra storage** Many backpack carriers also function as actual backpacks, with zippered compartments, pouches, and pockets for baby gear, water bottles, and other necessities.

◆ **Weather protection** Some come equipped with a canopy or cover to shield little passengers from sun, wind, and rain. (But don't forget sunblock and a hat if you're going to be toting your tot on a sunny day.)

CAR SEATS

OF ALL THE GEAR that you buy for your child, your choice of car seat will be the most important: It can make a life-or-death difference in a car crash. Every model of car seat made in the United States must meet federal safety standards, which helps to simplify shopping: Basically, any car seat you can buy has been rigorously safety-tested, so you don't need to weed out any potentially dangerous seats on your own—but you will have to consider other important criteria when selecting the seat. The top three:

1. YOUR CHILD'S AGE AND WEIGHT Different types of seats are designed for kids at specific ages and stages of development:

◆ **Infant seats** are rear-facing seats that consist of two parts: A base that stays secured in the car and the seat itself, which can be removed to double as a baby carrier. (A handle flips up for toting, and down and out of the way for riding.) They're designed to keep a baby in a reclining position at an angle that won't interfere with breathing and is safest in a crash. Infant seats are sometimes part of travel systems, meaning the car seat comes with a stroller that it fits into; some infant car seats that aren't part of a system are compatible with strollers anyway. Infant seats are for babies up to 22 pounds, although the **Graco Infant SafeSeat** ($190) will fit a baby up to 30 pounds and 32 inches, meaning you'll get a little more bang for your buck. The crème de la crème in this category may well be the **Britax Companion** ($160), which features head-protection pads. If you have a preemie,

▶ GIVE THE CAR SEAT CUSHION A GOOD FEEL BEFORE YOU BUY TO MAKE SURE THE SEAT IS WELL-PADDED, LIKE THIS EDDIE BAUER. DELUXE INFANT CAR SEAT (ABOUT $130).

GIZMOS & GADGETS

To keep your newborn's head steady as you (gently) round the bend, consider purchasing an infant head cushion—a soft u-shaped pad that fits inside car seats and strollers for extra head support. These can also be used in a bouncer seat early on when your baby is still a bit wobbly. There's **Infantino Total Head and Neck Support** (about $10) or the **Snuzzler Complete Head and Body Support for Any Seat by Kiddopotomus** (for about $18).

you might check out the **Chicco Key-Fit Infant Seat** ($150), which has a harness setting for the tiniest babies (and an angle adjuster that positions the seat perfectly with the push of a button).

◆ **Convertible seats** function as rear-facing infant seats for babies up to 30 or 35 pounds, then can be switched around to face forward for toddlers up to 40 pounds. (Some can accommodate kids up to 65 pounds.) When in the front-facing position, a convertible seat sits a child upright.

◆ **Booster seats** come equipped with a harness for a child between 20 and 40 pounds then can be used with the car's safety-restraints until he's 100 pounds.

▲ THE CORTINA DISCOVERY CAR SEAT ($280) HAS "MEMORY" RECLINE: IT REMEMBERS THE POSITION YOU LAST LEFT IT IN BEFORE FOLDING.

2. COMPATIBILITY WITH YOUR CAR As of September 2002, all new cars and car seats have been required to use the LATCH (Lower Anchors and Tethers for Children) system: The car seat has an anchor that hooks (or clamps) onto two rods (or bars) behind the seat cushion, and an upper tether secures the top, reducing whiplash and the risk of head injury. If your car is a 2003 or newer model, it will have the requisite rods to accommodate a new car seat, and installation will be relatively easy. If you have an older model car, see if you can retrofit it with the proper hardware, or else rely on the car's seat belt and, most likely, clamps to install the seat properly. Even if you have a LATCH system built into your car, however, you'll want to make sure the seat you buy is the right size and shape to

$KIP, $AVE, OR $PLURGE?

Is it safe to buy or borrow a used car seat? While we highly recommend that you buy new, if you're offered a secondhand seat for free, or you find a real bargain on one, make sure that it's never been in an accident. Even if it hasn't, look carefully for missing parts and cracks. If parts are missing, check with the manufacturer for replacements and request a copy of the seat's instructions. Also, contact the DOT Auto Safety Hotline, 888-327-4236, to find out if the seat has been recalled. (Be ready with the model number and date of manufacture, which is found on the seat.) You'll also find a list of all child seats that have been recalled since January 1990 at the National Highway Traffic Safety Administration's website (nhtsa.gov).

be installed safely. Buy from a store that will let you return a seat (in impeccable condition) if it doesn't fit properly.

3. SAFETY RESTRAINT SYSTEM   While you may come across a car seat with a 3-point harness, by far your safest option is one with a 5-point harness—meaning there are straps over each shoulder, each hip, and between your baby's legs. For an extra dose of safety, the **Britax Decathlon** ($285) has a crotch buckle that adjusts to three positions and tangle-proof straps. You may also encounter, on a forward-facing seat, a bar that crosses in front of your child's body rather than a seat belt; these bars are not considered safe and should be avoided.

Once you've narrowed down which type of car seat is right for your child, and which models will fit in your car, you can start considering other criteria, such as:

◆ **Appearance** Like everything else for babies, car seats are becoming increasingly sophisticated in style. One fun option for racing fans: **Graco's Simpson Ultra Cargo** ($140) is styled to look like a race-car seat.

▼ THE BRITAX DECATHALON TIFFANY SEAT ($285) IS ONE OF THE FEW CAR SEATS DESIGNED SPECIFICALLY FOR GIRLS.

If you plan to travel by airplane frequently during your baby's first 2 years, the **Sit-N-Stroll** car seat, which converts to a stroller (with a handle that pulls up and wheels that pop out of the bottom), can streamline the amount of gear you'll need. As a stroller, it's fine for short walks and great for maneuvering through an airport. It also makes for fuss-free transitions; if your baby falls asleep on the plane while strapped into the seat, you can just lift it up, pop out the wheels and push him over to the baggage claim. At about $220, it's a major investment—really only worth it for frequent fliers.

▲ GRACO SNUG-RIDE'S CLICK-ON STROLLER ADAPTER AND STAY-IN-CAR BASE ($150) CAN HELP MAKE A SMOOTH TRANSITION FROM CAR TO STROLLER.

◆ **Easy maintenance** Infants are as likely to spit up in their car seats as in their cribs, and toddlers are as likely to spill juice or crumble their crackers in their seats as their high chairs, so make sure you can remove the fabric easily (remember, you'll be maneuvering around all the safety straps) and pop it in the washer and dryer.

◆ **Stroller compatibility** This applies only to infant seats: If your car seat isn't part of a travel system, but you'd like to be able to push it around on wheels, make sure you have a stroller that will "accept" it.

◆ **Tote-ability** Be sure the handle on the infant seat you choose feels comfortable in your hand; some, like the **Graco Snug-Ride** ($150), are ergonomically designed.

◆ **Cup and snack holders** Many convertible car seats and toddler boosters sport soft pouches and pockets for sippy cups, toys, and other items; some even have retractable cup holders. Just make sure that your child can reach them easily.

◆ **Flight clearance** If you travel by air, be aware that the safest way for a baby to fly is secured in a car seat. (Many airlines now offer discounted fares or rebates for kids under 2 who fly in car seats.) Make sure that the seat you buy is approved for airline use.

◆ **Price** Most car seats cost around $100 to $150, but you'll find plenty that will set you back more (some Britax convertible car seats, which consistently receive stellar safety ratings, cost as much as $300). For less expensive models in all categories, check out Evenflo and Graco.

GIZMOS & GADGETS

If you travel by plane a lot and your child is at least a year old, you might want to invest in **CARES** ($75, including an instructional DVD; kidsflysafe.com), a harness that attaches directly to the airplane seat belt—see below). It's approved by the Federal Aviation Administration for kids who weigh 22 to 44 pounds (around 1 to 4 years old).

SLEEPING ARRANGEMENTS

IF YOUR TRAVELS INCLUDE an overnight stay somewhere, chances are you'll need a place for your baby to snooze. A portable crib or play yard that functions as a bassinet or crib will be an invaluable investment: It will fold up compactly and can be thrown in the trunk or checked as luggage if you're flying somewhere. Here's what to look for in each:

PORTABLE CRIBS

These look just like regular cribs—in miniature: They're about 35 percent smaller than standard baby beds. Although they're touted as great for travel, most people use them as a second crib rather than for overnights at Gran's house. But if you suspect that your child will feel more at home in a bed that resembles his regular one (rather than a play yard, which is the other option), or if you prefer putting your baby to bed in a crib that's higher off the ground when you're on the road, you might consider buying a portable crib. Keep the following features in mind:

◆ **Safety** A portable crib should meet the same safety standards as regular cribs:

1. slats that are no wider than $2\frac{3}{8}$ inches apart,

2. no cut outs that a small child could get his head or other body parts caught in (you're unlikely to encounter this unless you come across a very, very old used crib),

3. a sturdy, well-constructed wooden or metal frame,

4. a tight-fitting mattress. (Some portables are sold with a mattress; you can purchase one separately for about $20 if not.)

◆ **Versatility** Some portable cribs can be adjusted to more than one mattress height to accommodate babies at different ages and stages.

◆ **Wheels** For moving the crib from place to place within the house.

◆ **Compact size** It should be easy to carry and store when folded.

◆ **Easy to fold** Avoid lots of complicated latches.

154

◆ **Side rail that can be raised or lowered** This is not always an option, but it's nice one.

◆ **Appearance** Some wooden models come in a variety of finishes, if you want it to coordinate with your mother-in-law's guest room.

◆ **Price** Expect to pay between $80 and $180 for a portable crib, depending on brand, finish, and whether it has a mattress or not. (**NOTE:** You'll also need to buy specially sized sheets, labeled for portable cribs. This is important, as a regular crib sheet would be too loose and could pose a suffocation hazard to a newborn.)

▼ THE DELTA PORTABLE CRIB (ABOUT $120) ALSO CONVERTS TO A BASSINET.

PLAY YARDS

Some play yards (also popularly known as "pack-and-plays," although this is the brand name of many of the play yards made by Graco) are simply what the name suggests, a safe place to put a crawling or walking baby and a few toys (see pages 132–133 for more info on these types of play yards). The majority, however, double as cribs. Because of this multifunctional advantage over portable cribs, most parents choose one of these for overnight travel with a baby, though not all babies are content to sleep in one. In addition to the features listed on page 133, if you're using this as a crib, here are things to look for:

◆ **A removable bassinet** This is an insert that's only for babies who can't yet push up on their knees.

◆ **A removable changing table** Great for very small babies, but if you're buying for an older one or a toddler, skip it.

◆ **A snug-fitting mattress** Enough said.

◆ **A toy mobile** Again, only for very small babies; some play music.

▼ FULLY LOADED: THE SAHARA PLAY YARD (ABOUT $160; CHICCO) HAS JUST ABOUT EVERYTHING YOU NEED FOR OVERNIGHT TRIPS.

◆ **A night light** This can be a nice plus.

◆ **Storage** for diapers, wipes, etc. (when the play yard is set up).

◆ **A canopy** (to shield a sleeping baby from light; also comes in handy if you plan to use the play yard outdoors).

◆ **Room for two** Got twins? **Graco** makes a play yard with two bassinets ($185)—perfect for the early months. You'll need to spring for a second play yard once the babies outgrow the bassinet: It's not safe to put more than one child to sleep in a crib.

◆ **Safety rating** Look for a certification sticker from the Juvenile Products Manufacturers Association (JPMA).

◆ **Price** Depending on its features, expect to pay between $60 and $160 for a play yard.

◆ **Brand** You can't go wrong with a play yard by **Graco,** which produced the orginal **Pack 'N' Play** (the one that was mentioned most often in our survey) and now offers many variations on that theme. **Evenflo, Chicco, Fisher-Price,** and **Combi** have all followed suit with well-made, reliable play yards.

9

WHEELS

PICKING OUT A STROLLER needn't be a head-spinning experience: When push comes to shove, once you consider several important variables, you'll be able to narrow down your choices of carriages and strollers and pick out a set of wheels that will allow you and your child to roll merrily along.

Other moms in your neighborhood can be good source of information, and most moms are happy to talk about their strollers—it's a key purchase and a big part of life as a parent. Ask around to find out whether they like what they have (and why or why not).

STROLLERS

HOW TO CHOOSE A STROLLER

FIRST, CONSIDER WHERE YOU LIVE and the local terrain. A stroller that's going to be used on city streets will need different features than one that'll primarily see action in a suburban mall or on well-maintained sidewalks; and a stroller that will be used in a rural area will require yet another set of criteria if it's going to hold up over time. Because where you'll be using your stroller really drives what you need, we've organized our features list based on locale:

URBAN AREAS If you're a city dweller, you'll need to scale curbs, maneuver over sidewalk cracks and potholes, and fit between narrow store aisles, juggle your stroller and baby in and out of public transportation, perhaps lug them both up and down flights of stairs, and more. So your stroller should:

◆ **Be super-sturdy.** Not only is there the repeated jarring of broken sidewalks and such, there's some serious wear and tear due to the fact that urbanites do a lot of walking. In general, a steel frame will hold up much better than an aluminum one, but it'll be heavier—not so great if you live in a walk-up apartment building or use public transportation a lot. Your best bet: Find the lightest steel frame stroller that you can.

◆ **Sport rugged wheels.** You might consider a stroller that has air-filled tires, which give more easily on rough surfaces (and make for a smoother ride for little passengers). You'll also have an easier time bumping them up and down stairs. The downside is that they do need to be filled; so you might want to look for one that comes with a pump, or consider investing in a small pump.

▼ FANS OF THE HIGH-END BUGABOO CAMELEON STROLLER ($700) SAY ITS RUGGED WHEELS CAN TAKE BOTH BUMPY SIDEWALKS OR OFF-ROAD TERRAIN.

MOM-TESTED SURVEY!

24% of moms in our survey splurged on their strollers. The most popular brand: Graco, purchased by **66%** of the moms.

◆ **Fold compactly.** The stroller will need to fit inside the trunk of a taxicab as well as on public transportation. Lots of city moms in our survey swear by their lightweight, compact-fold **Maclaren** strollers, which come in several styles (click on the comparison chart at maclarenbaby.com to size each one up), ranging in price from around $110 to $250. Another urban fave: the **Inglesina Zippy** ($250): "We live in downtown Chicago, and have limited space.The Zippy folds up smaller than a bag of golf clubs!" raves one of our survey respondents.

◆ **Have ample storage space.** Since your stroller will serve as your baby's main means of transportation, make sure there's room in the basket for all his stuff as well for shopping bags and such. Also check to see that you have easy access to the basket if the seat back is reclined. (This is important wherever you live.)

▶ COMBO SEATING: GRACO MAKES POPULAR CAR SEAT/STROLLER SETS LIKE THIS MOSAIC TRAVEL SYSTEM (ABOUT $200).

SUBURBS Chances are, your stroller will primarily serve to get your child from the car to whatever your main destination is (the mall, the supermarket, the dry cleaners); beyond that, you'll mostly use it for walks around town or a stroll through your neighborhood to the park or a friend's house. A suburban baby's ride should:

◆ **Fit easily in the trunk of your car.** If you have a small trunk, ask while you're shopping if you can take the floor model out to your car to make sure it'll fit.

◆ **Work in tandem with a car seat.** This isn't absolutely necessary, but since you'll no doubt be spending lots of time in the car, a stroller that can accommodate an infant car seat (the type that clicks in and out of a base that stays strapped in the car), will be a boon. (Specific options are discussed on page 164–165.)

◆ **Be lightweight.** A heavy-duty—and therefore heavy—stroller shouldn't be necessary on the smooth floors of shopping malls and suburban sidewalks and streets. That said, not all towns can brag that their sidewalks and streets are crack- and pothole-free. If you're expecting your first baby, take a walk around your neighborhood and any other areas you expect to frequent with your baby in tow and check to see how beat up the pavement is before you stroller shop.

RURAL AREAS If you'll be strolling along unpaved roads, or live where there's lots of snow or on the beach, you'll most likely need an all-terrain stroller that features:

◆ **A heavy-duty suspension.** The stroller should take the switch from smooth pavement to rough road easily.

◆ **Large, air-filled tires.** These allow for a smoother ride that will both maintain the integrity of the stroller and be more comfortable for your baby. The big knobby wheels on **Phil & Ted's Sport** ($400) can conquer unpaved roads and grass hills with ease.

▼ OUR MOM-TESTERS LOVED THE VERSATILITY OF PHIL & TED'S SPORT ($400), WHICH CAN CARRY ONE OR TWO KIDS FROM INFANCY THROUGH TODDLERHOOD.

Mom Tip!

"Once I'd found the stroller I wanted in a store, I went online to compare prices and get the best deal. Sites like findstrollers.com and strollersfor-less.com linked me to the stores and sites that had my stroller for the cheapest price."

▲ THREE-WHEELED MODELS LIKE THE JEEP LIBERTY URBAN TERRAIN STROLLER ($100) ARE EASIER TO BUMP UP AND DOWN STEPS.

◆ **Shock absorbers.** Not always an option, but a nice one for super bumpy roads. Check out the smooth ride you get with the shock absorbers on the **Jeep Liberty Urban Terrain stroller** ($100; Kolcraft).

◆ **Accessories that accommodate the weather.** An ample sunshade for coastal climes, for example, or wind-and-precipitation protection for cold, wet environments—at least if you expect to be outside for any length of time.

NOTE: Some all-terrain strollers look like jogging strollers but aren't meant to be used as such. Don't run with a stroller that's not specifically made for that purpose, and keep in mind that a three-wheel stroller isn't as stable at any speed as one with four wheels.

NEXT, CONSIDER THE AGE OF YOUR BABY. Some types of strollers aren't safe or comfortable for infants under 6 months; others will only accommodate a child that young, leaving you to make a second stroller purchase once your baby hits the half-year mark. It is absolutely possible to buy one stroller to take you from your child's infancy through the toddler years, though you'll be looking for different features during these different stages. What you need to consider at each phase:

UNDER 6 MONTHS Because babies this age can't sit up, they shouldn't be propped into a standard stroller; they need a set of wheels that will let them ride fully reclined. The best options for a baby this young are:

◆ **Travel systems,** stroller/car seat combos that let you move the car seat from the car (the base stays strapped in) to the stroller, where it locks in place, usually with the baby facing toward you as you push. A baby can ride this way, kicked back in her car seat, for as long as she fits the seat—usually up to 22 pounds. You'll appreci-ate the spacious shopping basket on the **Cortina Travel System Stroller** (Chicco; $300), and the one-handed fold/unfold mechanism.

◆ **Strollers that can be used with car seats** from different manufacturers, so you can create your own travel system using the seat of your choice. In this category, we like the **Zooper Waltz** ($200).

◆ **Seat carrier frames,** which are frames that accommodate most car seats: just click the seat in place. Most feature a basket and many also sport conveniences like a tray and cup holder. They're lightweight, but you'll have to switch to a regular stroller once your baby outgrows her car seat. **Kolcraft's Snap-N-Go Universal Car Seat Carrier** ($50) is easy to haul in out of your trunk and narrow enough to navigate store aisles. It also comes in a style that can hold two car seats. (A must-have for one of the moms in our survey, who said, "Even though you can only use it for a short time, I would highly recommend the Snap-N-Go Double Stroller to anyone with twins.") **Baby Trend's Snap-N-Go Double Stroller/car seat** carriers start at around $80.

◆ **Convertible stroller/carriages** with backrests that recline all the way back for infants; once a baby is able to sit up, it can be adjusted to a standard stroller configuration. An important safety note when considering a convertible stroller: Make sure that there's a mechanism for closing off the leg holes when the stroller's reclined in carriage position, to prevent the baby from slipping through. We like **Combi's Savvy Soho DX** ($90) and the **Peg Perego Venezia** ($370), which has a reversible handle, full recline seat, and detachable fabric boot.

◀ AT 16 POUNDS, THE ZOOPER WALTZ ($200) IS ALMOST AS LIGHT AS AN UMBRELLA STROLLER.

165

GIZMOS & GADGETS

Can't imagine leaving home without your iPod? Some strollers feature a special holder for an MP3 player, like the **iBaby Umbrella Stroller** ($50; Kolcraft).

♦ **High-end strollers** One brand of super-expensive stroller, the **Bugaboo** ($700), has become more popular in recent years, partly due to the celebrities who are frequently photographed pushing them around. The Bugaboo, which comes in three models—the **Frog,** the **Gekko** (an all-terrain design), and the **Chameleon** (which lets you put together a two-toned stroller of your own design)—features a removable bassinet for the infant stage and fits kids up to 45 pounds. Fans rave about the stroller's maneuverability, especially on urban streets. Even pricier, the **Stokke Xplory** ($950) has a removable bassinet and the stroller can be adjusted so that a child faces either forward or back.

OVER 6 MONTHS Once a baby can sit up on her own, the options include:

♦ **Standard strollers** These can be anything from lightweight models with minimal creature comforts to roomier, heavier strollers with plenty of bells and whistles for mother and child. Price range: $60 to more than $800.

♦ **Umbrella strollers** They have curved handles (hence the name), are super-light—the **Chicco Capri** (about $60) weighs just 15 pounds— and fold up very compactly. Some are little more than fabric attached to a frame and may not be very comfortable for lengthy rides; these are fine as second strollers (perfect in an airport, for example) and cheap—as little as $14 to $20. But for a stroller that boasts both umbrella convenience and a smooth ride, check out the **Silver Cross Micro V2** ($130). It has a removable seat cushion and canopy to give it a carriage-like feel without the bulk.

♦ **All-terrain strollers** Because they're designed to go from one surface to another, these have fat, air-filled tires. Some have a three-wheel design, and the front wheel can be locked for stability on rough surfaces.

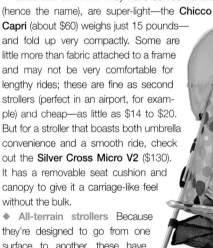

◄ DREAM RIDE: THIS COMBI TWIN SAVVY STROLLER CAN HOLD BOTH A CAR SEAT AND A TODDLER.

DOUBLE STROLLERS

If you're looking for a double stroller (because you're expecting twins or to accommodate a newborn and an older sibling), keep these options in mind:

SIDE-BY-SIDE STROLLERS are just what they sound like—strollers with two seats next to each other, both facing forward. Most side-by-side strollers are designed to accommodate children of the same age and size, so they're best for twins or siblings who are very close in age.

Only one company makes a side-by-side that can accommodate a car seat: **Combi's Twin Savvy** stroller accepts the **Combi Connection** infant car seat, which is sold separately ($280 for the stroller; $160 for the car seat). One mother of twins in our survey raved about her **Peg Perego Aria Twin** stroller, which runs around $300 to $350. If you consider a side-by-side, make sure it's narrow enough to fit through standard doorways. Several moms spoke highly of the compact double stroller by **Maclaren**, loving that both seats recline and that it's easy to maneuver and fold.

TANDEM STROLLERS Tandems are constructed with one seat behind the other. Typically, the rear seat reclines, making them the ideal choice for an infant and toddler. Other models allow kids to ride facing each other, or, like the **Evenflo Take Me Too Double Stroller** ($90–$140), have "stadium seating": The rear seat is positioned slightly higher than the front one to give the kid in the back a view of what's ahead. Tandems are a little harder to maneuver up curbs, but are the same width as single strollers so they fit easily through doorways. **Phil and Ted's E3** has a second seat option ($380) and is a good, versatile, and fairly compact choice if you have a baby and a toddler.

STAND-ON TANDEMS These have a platform for your older child to stand on, rather than a full seat. **Joovy's Caboose Stand-On Tandem** ($165) also has a rear bench and a universal car seat attachment.

▲ SHOPPING WITH YOUR STROLLER? A TANDEM STROLLER, LIKE THE ALL TERRAIN TANDEM FROM EDDIE BAUER ($240), FITS THROUGH STORE AISLES MORE EASILY THAN A DOUBLE MODEL.

OTHER THINGS TO CONSIDER Once you've narrowed down the type of stroller you want to shop for, keep in mind that the best way to select a stroller is to test-drive it: Go to a store that has plenty of brands and styles on display and check out all the options. You can always buy (or at least shop for the best price) online, or list the stroller of your choice on your baby registry, if that's more convenient.

◄ STROLL-ERS WITH A PLATFORM LIKE THIS JOOVY CABOOSE ($165) ARE PERFECT IF YOU HAVE A BABY AND TODDLER OR PRE-SCHOOLER. THE "BIG" KID CAN EITHER STAND FACING FORWARD OR SIT FACING BACKWARDS.

$KIP, $AVE, OR $PLURGE?

There's something romantic about a real baby carriage—the kind of buggy with big wheels that's made just for infants. But unless you're a celeb mom with unlimited funds, investing in one doesn't make a whole lot of sense. There are plenty of more economical options for the short period during which your child will need to be toted around on her back before she's ready to sit up in a standard stroller. Our advice: If you want a real carriage, see if you can find one to borrow or consider buying it used (make sure it's in supreme condition and isn't a model that's been recalled).

Here's what to consider when shopping for a stroller:

◆ **Stability and durability** Jiggle the stroller gently. Whether the frame is made of lightweight aluminum or heavy-duty steel, it should feel sturdy and solid. One particularly durable model: the **Compass S300 Deluxe Stroller** ($140), which uses steel (instead of plastic) in the posts that hold the wheels.

◆ **Maneuverability** Push the stroller around. It should move smoothly and be able to take corners tightly. If you expect to encounter lots of curbs, practice tilting the front wheels up. Try pushing with one hand as well.

◆ **A safety restraint** Don't opt for anything less than a 5-point harness.

◆ **An easy open-and-close mechanism** Ideally, you should be able to open, close, and lift a stroller with one hand (since your other will often be holding your baby).

◆ **A comfortable handle height** You should be able to push the stroller with your elbows bent comfortably. If you can't find a stroller with fixed handles that fit you, or if your spouse or caregiver will also be behind your baby's wheels, look for one with handles that adjust up and down to accommodate all users.

◆ **Leg room for you** The stroller should be constructed so that as you walk behind it you don't have to shorten your step to avoid kicking the back of it. Statuesque moms may especially appreciate **Graco's Metrolite** ($150): If your stride is long, it won't leave you with bruised shins.

◆ **Cup holders** or trays for you and/or your child. Many strollers have a tray that spans the width of the handles with an indentation to fit a bottle of water or cup of Joe. Standard strollers sometimes have a similar set up for an upright-sitting child for keeping snacks and toys and within easy reach.

◆ **Protection from the elements for your baby** Make sure the canopy folds down far enough to truly shade her eyes and keep her dry in a moderate downpour.

◆ **Ample storage** Steer clear of skimpy under-seat baskets, especially if you expect to use your stroller for shopping or lengthy outings that require you to bring along a lot of stuff. Be sure you can access the basket easily with the seat reclined, or if the stroller is part of a travel system, when the car seat is attached.

▼ THE METRO-LITE STROLLER FROM GRACO ($150) IS A GOOD CHOICE FOR LONG-LEGGED MOMS AND DADS.

◀ THE HANDLE ON THE S300 DELUXE STROLLER BY COMPASS ($140) IS REVERSIBLE, SO YOU CAN PUSH THE STROLLER WITH YOUR BABY FACING FORWARD OR BACKWARD.

◆ **Easy upkeep** Check to see the fabric can be washed or wiped down—it's going to be splattered with everything from spit-up to mud to ground-in Cheerio crumbs.

◆ **Warranty** Because most manufacturers will require that you bring the stroller back to the store or send it to them (you'll pay the postage) for repair, it's best to buy from a store, catalog, or Web site that guarantees your money back if the stroller malfunctions.

◆ **Certification** Both the American Society for Testing and Material (ASTM) and the Juvenile Products Manufacturers Association (JPMA) have voluntary certification programs. Not all stroller-makers participate (the ones that do are Baby Trend, Britax, Bugaboo, Delta, Dorel, Evenflo, Graco, Hauck Fund for Kids, J. Mason, Kolcraft, Maclaren, and Peg Perego). Strollers made by other companies may be perfectly fine (strollers are tested for safety belts, brakes, leg openings, and locking mechanisms that prevent accidental folding, plus stability and lack of sharp edges), but certification does add an extra degree of insurance that the stroller is safe and reliable.

JOGGING STROLLERS

◀ BABY JOGGER: THE ORIGINAL AND STILL MOST POPULAR BRAND OF JOGGING STROLLER (FROM $250 TO $550)

THESE ARE SPECIALLY DESIGNED to ride steady at faster-than-walking speeds. They sport:

◆ three 12- to 20-inch all-terrain, air-filled tires (smaller tires are fine for fast walking, larger ones are best for running)

◆ a wide profile to prevent tipping

◆ a lightweight frame

The first thing to know about buying one is that they're not safe for infants who don't have the neck strength and head control to withstand being bumped and jarred. Get your workouts in solo until your baby is 6 months old. Then, besides the general advice for shopping for a stroller, look for the following details:

◆ **Handle height** is key. When you rest your hand on the handlebar, your forearm should be perpendicular to it. Adjustable-height handles are great if more than one person will be using the stroller.

◆ **Easy to fold** Joggers can be cumbersome, so if you expect that you'll be hauling yours in the car, look for one that folds easily, like the **Baby Jogger Q-Series** ($300): It folds in half with the lift of a strap.

◆ **A 5-point harness system** is a must.

◆ **A hand brake** lets you make quick stops and control your speed down hills.

◆ **A safety cord** that attaches to your wrist. This prevents the stroller (with your child!) from getting away from you.

◆ **Wheel locks** keep the stroller still while you're getting your child in and out of her seat.

◆ **Arm guards** are like "wings" on either side of the seat—protect little hands and fingers.

◆ **Fenders** prevent little toes from grazing the wheels or spokes.

◆ **A sunshade** One of the moms in our survey gave a double thumbs-up to her **BOB Jogging Stroller** for its large sunshade (and "compactability"). BOB jogging strollers cost between $280 and $400 and up to $550 for a double model (bobstrollers.com for stores).

◀ THE BOB IRONMAN JOGGING STROLLER ($490 FOR A DOUBLE; $350 FOR A SINGLE) IS THE OFFICAL STROLLER OF THE IRONMAN TRIATHALON.

173

GIZMOS & GADGETS

Let's say you fall in love with a stroller, but it's missing one or two little features you'd love to have. There are myriad accessories you can buy to pimp your baby's ride. Some to consider:

◆ **Extra storage**
If your stroller's basket is skimpy, look for a bag that will give you more room for toting. Make sure that you buy a bag that won't tip your stroller back-wards when your child isn't inside to weigh it down. One we like: the **Dadgear Backpack** ($92).

◆ **Bottle holder** On longer outings, you may need to keep a cool one on hand for your baby: **J.L. Childress** makes several types of insu-lated stroller-holders for bottles and baby food jars. **The Stroller Cooler** ($13) even has a pocket for your water bottle, and a hidden pouch for money or keys.

174

◆ **Rain cover** This is a clear plastic cover that keeps the wind, rain, and cold off of your baby. It should cover the stroller completely, so that your child's feet and sides stay warm and dry, and have perforations for air circulation. You can often buy a rain cover made specifically for your stroller: if so, that's your best bet for a good seal. If not, **JPS Juvenile Products Rain Covers** ($10) come in several sizes to fit different stroller types.

175

◆ **Cupholder** These usually clip onto a stroller's handles; some are simple cup-shaped holders, while others are part of a more intricate add-on, like **Kel-Gar's Stroll'r Hold'r** ($6), which sports three hooks along with the cupholder. Make sure that the one you shop for is designed to fit your stroller's handles: Some can accommodate only horizontal or vertical handles, while others work with both.

◆ **Buggy board** For older sibs who are too big for a stroller but still need a chance to rest their little feet, one of these attachable platforms-on-wheels can be a savior. The **Buggy Board Maxi** (about $90; Regal Lager) is easy to connect and disconnect and is height-adjustable. If you have a three-wheeled stroller (with a rear-wheel axle), you'll need the **Kiddy Board** (about $60; Lascal) which easily attaches to the rear axle.

◆ **Hooks** Attached to a stroller's handles, these can be used to hold your purse, diaper bag, or groceries. **Kel-Gar Stroll'r Swivel'r** hooks swivel 360 degrees ($3.99 for a pack of two).

176

◆ **Bunting bag** These little co-coons fit inside a stroller (or car seat) and zip up to the chin to create a warm, cozy nest—so you don't have to bother with a bulky snowsuit: You can just zip your warmly dressed baby into her bunting before you leave the house, and she'll stay toasty. (Don't forget her mittens and hat, though!) Look for a warm interior (fleece or microsuede are ideal) and a wind- and water-resistant exterior. **Bundle Me** buntings (from $25) come in a variety of styles, colors, and weights.

◆ **Sun shade** This can be as simple as an umbrella that attaches to the side of the stroller, or as intricate as the UV-protective shades made by **Protect-a-Bub** (shown at right; $39 and up, depending on size and type of stroller) and **Kiddopotamus** ($15 for single-stroller shade, $25 for double-stroller shade).

10
SAFETY
GEAR

HILDPROOFING YOUR HOME isn't just essential for safeguarding your baby: It's important for your own peace of mind. The safer your child's surroundings and the more familiar you are with potential household dangers and how to prevent them, the easier it will be for you to relax and enjoy your time with your family.

That said, all the outlet covers and cabinet locks in the world can't replace vigilance, so consider these items as tools to help make your home safe—not replacements for your watchful eye.

The best way to approach childproofing is both room-by-room, and age-by-age. Each area of your home presents particular potential dangers, and each stage of development will allow your child to get into more trouble. **Get down at kid's-eye level and go through your entire house, looking for potential hazards.** You'll need to repeat this process as your child develops: What's dangerous for a crawler will be different from what can hurt a walker.

MUST-HAVE SAFETY GEAR

KEEP THIS LIST of must-haves by your side when you go to buy childproofing items. You can find many of them, such as outlet covers, at your local supermarket, drugstore, or hardware store, as well as at baby stores and chain department stores. Some useful sites for childproofing products: safety1st.com, safebeginnings.com, perfectlysafe.com, and kidco.com (for safety gates and window guards).

You may not need everything on the checklist, depending on the configuration of your home and your child's age, but it's a good, comprehensive roundup, and will help make sure that you buy only what you need.

180

SAFETY GEAR CHECKLIST

WHAT	WHERE
Smoke detectors	One in or near each bedroom and near the kitchen
Carbon monoxide detectors	One in or near each bedroom and near the kitchen
Regular fire extinguisher	In the garage
Compact, one-time use fire extinguisher	In the kitchen
Lower cabinet and drawer locks	On cabinets and drawers where dangerous items might be stored.
Stove knob covers	On all stove and oven knobs
Oven lock	On oven door
Toilet seat lock(s)	On all toilet lids
Tub spout cover	On all bathtub spouts
Antiscald devices	On sink faucets
Corner and edge bumpers	On the corners of coffee tables and raised fireplace hearths
Hardware-mounted gate	At the top of stairs
Pressure-mounted gate	At the bottom of stairs and certain doorways
Railing netting or plastic guards	Stair railings
Furniture straps or brackets	On to the wall behind heavy furniture
Outlet plate covers	For all outlets, especially those near sinks
Power strip covers	On all power strips
Window blind cord wraps	On any window with long blind cords
Window guards	On any upstairs windows that don't lock securely
Door knob or lever covers	On the doors to any off-limits areas

181

► AN EASY WAY TO REMEMBER WHEN TO CHANGE SMOKE-ALARM BATTERIES: REPLACE THEM WHEN YOU SWITCH YOUR CLOCKS IN THE SPRING AND FALL.

◆ **Smoke and carbon monoxide detectors** There should be one in or near each bedroom, and one near the kitchen. One family-friendly idea: the **Vocal Smoke Alarm** ($30; signalonesafety.com) lets you record a message, which alternates with a siren. (Research shows that Mom's voice is more effective than traditional alarms.) You can also find combo smoke and carbon monoxide detectors. Whatever model you choose, be sure to replace batteries every six months.

◆ **Fire extinguisher** Besides a regular extinguisher, it's a good idea to keep a compact, one-time use version in the kitchen, like **First Alert's Tundra Fire Suppressant** ($20; firstalert.com). It'll put out small household fires, including cooking oil flare-ups.

◄ TUNDRA'S FIRE SUPPRESSANT FOAM ($20) IS BIODEGRADABLE AND NONTOXIC.

182

◆ **Lower cabinet and drawer locks** (ideally, move any dangerous items, like knives or cleaners, to higher storage). We especially like the **KidCo Adhesive Mount Magnet Lock Starter Set** ($16; kidco.com) for its easy installation (no tools needed!); a magnetic key gives you—but not your child—easy access to cabinets and drawers.

◆ **Stove knob covers** (to prevent little hands from turning on a burner). Also remember to cook on the rear burners and turn pot handles toward the back so that your child can't reach them.

◆ **Oven lock**

◆ **Toilet seat locks**

◆ **Tub spout cover** (set your hot water heater to 120 degrees, or buy anti-scald devices—for around $100—and install on faucets). One cute option: a turtle-shaped **Spout Protector** ($5; summerinfant.com).

183

GIZMOS & GADGETS

To help prevent both slips and burns in the bathtub, line the bottom with non-skid decals. In this set, one of the ten decals turns from blue to magenta when the water temperature edges above 98°F (37°C). **Mommy's Helper Tub Water Temps** ($4 for ten; Mommy's Helper).

▲ WHETHER YOU'RE CARRYING PRECIOUS CARGO OR STRUGGLING WITH GROCERY BAGS, YOU'LL APPRECIATE A BABY GATE WITH A FOOT PEDAL, LIKE THIS ONE FROM THE FIRST YEARS ($50).

◆ **Corner and edge bumpers** These are a must on coffee table corners and raised fireplace hearths. Your child might try to pull them off, but give them a try.

◆ **Gates** Use a hardware-mounted style at top of stairs; a pressure-mounted style is okay at bottom of stairs. Look for one that you can operate while holding your baby or a laundry basket: The **Hands-Free Gate** by The First Years ($50; learningcurve.com) opens with a foot pedal.

◆ **Railing netting or plastic guards** if you have an open railing—keeps kids from slipping through.

◆ **Furniture straps or brackets** to attach to the wall any heavy furniture that could be pulled over.

◆ **Outlet plate covers** These are safer than simple plugs, which an industrious toddler could pry out all too easily. In particular, you need to protect outlets near the sink from water. Those in the bathroom (and kitchen) should have ground-fault circuit-interrupters (GFCI), which turn off the power source if they get wet. If your older home doesn't have these, look for GFCI wall plates at home stores. They come in different finishes to match your décor. One we like: **Baldwin Classic Design GFCI Wallplates** (from $6 for a single wallplate, $10 for a double; homedepot.com).

◆ **Power strip covers**

◆ **Window blind cord wraps** You can also cut blind cords short or replace blinds with shades. Go to windowcoverings.org for information on how to order and install free cord stops, tassels, and tie-down devices to retrofit window blind cords made before 2001.

◆ **Window guards or window stops** Use window guards if your windows don't lock securely. Make sure that there's no more than four inches between the bars of the window guard and that one window per room can be easily used for escape during a fire.

◆ **Door knob or lever covers** (for any off-limits areas). You'll appreciate the unobtrusiveness of **Safety 1st Clear Grip Door Knob Covers:** They're see-through ($3 for two; safety1st.com).

$KIP, $AVE, OR $PLURGE?

Heightened concern for child safety in the home has set off a wave of professional childproofers and childproofing businesses. Should you spring for one? It's probably not necessary, if you follow the advice in this chapter. However, if you're too overwhelmed, feel you need help installing things correctly, or have a home that makes installation challenging, by all means seek professional help. Expect to pay anywhere from several hundred to several thousand dollars, depending on where you live, the size of your home, and the extent of the job. To find a childproofer, ask your friends who have had their homes childproofed, or visit the International Association for Child Safety website (iafcs.com) or look in the Yellow Pages under "safety consultants."

11
TOYS & FUN

PHEW! You've picked out the perfect stroller, the safest car seat, the classiest crib, and the cutest outfits. Now it's time to stock the toy chest! Picking out toys (and other fun stuff) can seem like anything but child's play at first, given the vast variety and the pressure to buy things that are "educational." Don't let that ruin your fun: We're here to help.

Each year, *Parenting* magazine's editors vet hundreds of new toys, then have moms and kids around the country test them to find the ones that are the most fun (our top criteria), that are safe, hold up well with repeated play, aren't too loud, etc. The winners are published in the November issue, in a special Mom-Tested Toys of the Year section.

Parenting regularly picks out great books, toys, DVDs, software, and CDs throughout the year. You'll find buying guides for each of these categories of kids' entertainment at parenting.com; the info is updated regularly to include new selections.

TOYS

DESPITE THE HELPFUL guidance you'll find in print, online, and from friends, we guarantee you're going to want to do some toy-shopping yourself. Use the following criteria as you shop for playthings and other baby entertainment—but, most important, let what seems most fun to you and your baby be your guide.

Since a child's age and developmental stage are key to the type of toys that will be safest and most appropriate for her, select toys accordingly. Use the packaging info as a guide. According to the Toy Industry Association, toys are age-graded based on the following criteria: safety factors, the average ability of a child that age to manipulate the toy and understand how to play with it, and the interests of that child.

So no matter how brilliant your little one may be, if the label says the toy is for ages 3 and up, it means 3 and up. Giving a toddler a toy meant for an older child may be a choking or other safety risk. Plus, she'll only get frustrated if the toy is beyond her abilities.

▲ CUTE CRITTER: THE TWISTY BUG FROM BRIGHT STARTS ($6.99) HAS BOTH BRIGHT COLORS AND INTERESTING TEXTURES TO DELIGHT A BABY.

AGES BIRTH TO 1½

Babies are fascinated by their environment, and they learn a lot just by observing their caregivers and siblings: A simple game of watch-Mommy-pick-up-my-spoon-every-time-I-drop-it-from-the-highchair is a valuable lesson in cause and effect, for instance. Here's a chart of the skills and milestones babies are working on during their first 18 months, followed by the types of toys that will help them:

SKILL(S)	TOYS THAT HELP DEVELOP SKILLS
Tracking objects Discovering where sounds come from	Mobiles, mirrors, soft books Rattles and other items that make noises—squeaks, beeps, crinkles, animal sounds, etc.
Hand-eye coordination Cause-and-effect	Activity centers (sometimes called busy boxes) Tables (with several types of playthings) Stacking toys
Physical skills, like grasping, sitting, crawling, and rolling over	Push- and pull-toys

188

When buying a toy for a baby, consider the following criteria:

◆ **Size and weight** The number one way that a baby plays is by picking things up, so her toys should be lightweight and small enough for her to grasp.

◆ **Grasp-ability** Look for soft toys, or ones that have handles, protrusions, or finger holes. Make sure any buttons, levers, or knobs are easy for little hands to manage.

◆ **Texture** Offer your child a variety of materials—wood, cloth, plastic—and textures. Lots of baby toys feature, say, a rough patch of nubby fabric, a smooth side, and a few raised dots. The best infant ones also match different textures to visual cues: A fabric ball might have a panel of smooth red satin and a rough corduroy panel in blue.

◆ **Sound effects** Whenever possible, look for toys that connect a sound to an action: When your baby shakes a rattle harder, the clacking should grow louder too.

◆ **Color** No need to focus on black, white, and red toys—even for infants. A pure visual diet of high-contrast colors will no doubt bore you both.

◆ **Appearance** Infants love colors and bold patterns, mirrors, and glitter. They don't necessarily love bright flashing lights and toys that blink like a Las Vegas gambling hall—even though playthings that do this abound. Use your own instincts as a guide; if a toy is annoying to you, chances are it'll be overstimulating for your baby as well (in any case, you're not going to want it around the house).

◆ **Interactivity** Make sure your baby can make the toy beep or tumble; she should be an active participant, not a passive observer.

◆ **Versatility** You'll get more bang for your buck with a toy that can be played with in more than one way—for instance, a push-toy that can also be pulled.

◆ **Educational value** Forget about it! Toys that feature numbers and letters won't give your infant an advantage at this stage. Choose playthings that are fun and that you'll enjoy together.

▼ EACH SEGMENT OF THE 6-FOOT-LONG GUND PLUSH CATERPILLAR ($110) MAKES A DIFFERENT SOUND WHEN YOUR BABY SQUEEZES IT. ALSO IN A SMALLER VERSION (17 INCHES LONG; $9).

TINKLE · CRINKLE · RATTLE · SQUEAK

A NOTE ABOUT RECALLS:

To check on recalled and dangerous toys, go to Parenting.com/recalls. You'll get updates from the U.S. Consumer Product Safety Commission (CPSC) and toy manufacturers.

◆ **Skill level** Your child will pass through many stages of development during her first 18 months, meaning her abilities will change rapidly. Try to match the toys you offer her at any given time with her skills, but keep in mind that it's okay to let her try out one that's one step beyond her present abilities if you can help and she can imitate you.

◆ **Safety** Avoid any toy that's small enough to fit inside of your child's mouth: In fact, anything that can fit inside an empty toilet paper roll is considered unsafe for a child under 3. The strings on pull-toys should be no more than 6 inches long. Make sure the toy is well constructed, with no small parts that are likely to get loose and come off.

◆ **Durability** A toy that will see a lot of playtime should be washable or wipeable, and well made.

◆ **Brand** Companies that make consistently entertaining, safe, and developmentally appropriate toys for babies include Fisher-Price, Lamaze, ALEX, Leapfrog (specializing in electronic toys), Playskool, Little Tikes, Step2, iPlay, Corolle (for baby dolls), and Sassy (all available wherever toys are sold, from national toy chains like Toys 'R' Us to Target and KMart); and Brio, Manhattan Toy, Chicco, Infantino, HABA, Small World Toys, and Tiny Love—typically carried by small, independent toy stores, as well as online.

▲ THE BRIGHT COLORS, EASY-TO-GRASP DESIGN, AND CHEWABLE TEXTURE HAVE MADE FIRST KEYS FROM THE FIRST YEARS A HIT SINCE 1940 ($1.50).

▲ COBBLER'S BENCH TOYS, LIKE THIS ONE FROM SCHYLLING ($12.99) CAN HELP DEVELOP FINE MOTOR SKILLS.

AGES 1½ TO 3

Toddlers are on the go, all the time. Here's a chart of the skills and discoveries they are working on from about 18 months to 3 years, followed by the types of toys that will help them develop:

SKILL(S)	TOYS THAT HELP DEVELOP SKILLS
Fine motor skills	Crayons, modeling clay, lacing toys, peg boards, shape sorters, simple puzzles, building blocks, bath, sand, and water toys
Gross motor skills	Ride-on and push-toys, soft balls
Discovering how the "real" world works (and imitating Mom and Dad)	Puppets, baby dolls, toy phones, tools, cooking apparatus
Figuring out rhythm	Musical toys, like keyboards

$KIP, $AVE, OR $PLURGE?

Should you buy used toys? Certainly, as long as they're in good condition. Look for ripped seams on soft toys (where small parts could be exposed), splinters or chipped paint on wooden toys, and rust on outdoor playthings. (Toss out any of your own toys that wind up in similar condition.) Otherwise, any item that looks new or almost-new, is age-appropriate, and has all its pieces is fair game. You're especially likely to get good deals on baby and toddler toys at yard sales and secondhand shops: Playthings for these age groups often see little wear and tear, given how quickly kids develop and move on from one interest and set of abilities to another.

When buying a toy for an older baby or toddler, keep these factors in mind:

◆ **Durability** Toddlers are tough on toys—they'll throw them, stand on them, bang them on the floor. Choose items made of thick plastic, wood, or tough, machine-washable fabric. Keep an eye out for parts that might break off or come off easily; choking is still an issue for this age group.

▼ A KIDS' FAVORITE FOR 50 YEARS: THE FISHER-PRICE CORN POPPER ($16)

◆ **Quality** Make sure the toy easily does what it claims to. Do the stacking cups stay stacked? Does the handle crank smoothly? Do the pieces fit through the shape sorter without a glitch?

◆ **Attention span** Toddlers thrive on quick results, so look for playthings that do something immediate, like a pop-up toy that springs to life with the push of a button. Forget electronic toys that keep doing their thing until they run through a full cycle. Bor-ing!

◆ **Educational value** Don't worry about the ABCs, and opt instead for items that help a child think and play imaginatively, like art materials, blocks, and pretend tea sets.

◆ **Brand** The companies listed on the previous page make toys for toddlers as well. You'll also find terrific toys for this age group from LEGO, MegaBloks, and Playmobil.

191

▲ BABY EINSTEIN COLOR KALEIDO-SCOPE ($15)

▲ FISHER-PRICE SNAP AND LOCK BEADS ($5)

CLASSICS

These playthings for little kids have made *Parenting*'s Toy Hall of Fame in recent years, based on their timeless ability to entertain and teach (for the most current list, go to parenting.com):

FOR AGES 0 TO 1½:
- ◆ Gund Plush Caterpillar ($7 for an 8-inch model; Gund)
- ◆ Galt Pop-Up Toy ($15; Galt)
- ◆ First Blocks ($10; Fisher-Price)
- ◆ Whoozit ($10–$20; Manhattan Toy Company)
- ◆ Brio Twin Rattles ($6; Brio)
- ◆ Stacking cups (various companies)
- ◆ Snap-Lock Beads ($5; Fisher-Price)
- ◆ Gymini Playmat ($50; Tiny Love)
- ◆ First Keys (about $2; various companies)
- ◆ Infant Stim-Mobile ($20)
- ◆ Gymfinity Baby Gym ($30)
- ◆ Chatter Telephone ($5; Fisher-Price)
- ◆ Rock-A-Stack ($5; Fisher-Price)
- ◆ Skwish ($15; Manhattan Toy Company)

▼ MANHATTAN TOY COMPANY SKWISH ($15)

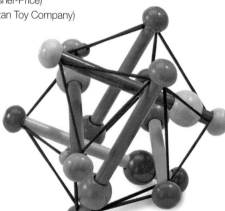

▲ BRIGHT STARTS JIGGLING GIRAFFE TEETHER ($5)

▲ RADIO FLYER WAGON ($90)

FOR AGES 1½ TO 3:

◆ Jack-in-the-Box ($15–$30; various companies)
◆ Cabbage Patch Kids dolls ($30–$35; Cabbage Patch Kids)
◆ ImagiBRICKS (about $30)
◆ Sit 'N Spin ($20; Playskool)
◆ See 'N Say (about $10; Fisher-Price)
◆ Raggedy Ann doll ($10–$20; Raggedy Ann)
◆ Shape-O ($25; circular shape sorter by Tupperware)
◆ Alphabet Blocks (about $10–$20; various companies)
◆ Mr. Potato Head ($6; Playskool)
◆ Little People School Bus ($17; Fisher-Price)
◆ Corn Popper push-toy ($10; Fisher-Price)
◆ Supermaze ($45; Educo)
◆ Cobbler's Bench ($6–$20; various companies)
◆ Radio Flyer Red Wagon ($90; Radio Flyer)

▲ JACK-IN-THE-BOX FROM SCHYLLING ($13)

▼ MR. POTATO HEAD ($6)

▼ IMAGIBRICKS (ABOUT $30)

193

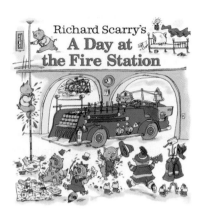

WE KNOW, WE KNOW, at the ripe old age of 6 weeks, or 4 months, or 2 years, your child is hardly reading yet. But books are bound to be an essential part of her development from the minute she gnaws on her first copy of *Goodnight Moon*. To help you start filling her bookshelves, and nurture a life-long love of reading, here's what to look for when buying books for babies and toddlers:

◆ **Durability** Board books are best for young babies, who are as likely to chew on them as look at them. Small, chunky books are easiest for little hands to manipulate; older babies and toddlers can graduate to thinner board books, and even books with regular pages if they aren't likely to rip them.

◆ **Options for exploration** Shiny surfaces, different textures, and pieces that move or make noises are very appealing to babies, even if you find them gimmicky.

◆ **Illustrations of familiar objects** A ball, a cat, a Mommy, another baby—babies love to see things from their world in the pages of books. Photos of everyday items—like those found in Dorling-Kindersley board books (dk.com)—are especially likely to captivate a tot.

◆ **Words per page** Books with no words or just one to two per page, are best for babies, who won't sit still for complicated plots; however, toddlers can start to understand very, very simple stories. In fact, books with little text that allow you to tell the story your own way are ideal. Some classic examples: *Goodnight, Gorilla* by Peggy Rathman and *Hug* by Jez Alborough.

Mom Tip!

"To help my baby develop a love of books, I keep her board books in a basket with her other toys, rather than on a bookshelf, so she can always reach them."

♦ **Repetition** Toddlers love to hear words and phrases repeated over and over again. Books like *Chicka Chicka Boom Boom* by Bill Martin Jr., John Archambault, and Lois Ehlert; *We're Going on a Bear Hunt* by Helen Oxenbury and Michael Rosen; and anything by Eric Carle or Dr. Seuss, are likely to make a young child's ears perk up.

PARENTING PICKS: BOOKS

This list represents some of our favorite Mom-Tested books for babies and toddlers. You can use it (and the list of classic baby and toddler books and authors that follows), to start building a beloved collection for your child's library.

BIRTH TO 18 MONTHS:
♦ **Baby Animals; Baby Talk** by Harriet Ziefert; illustrated by SAMI ($9 each; Blue Apple)
♦ **Belly Button Book** by Sandra Boynton ($7; Workman)
♦ **Diddle, Diddle, Dumpling** by Tracey Campbell Pearson ($6; Farrar, Straus, and Giroux)
♦ **Look at the Animals!** by Peter Linenthal ($7; Dutton)
♦ **This Little Piggy** edited by Jane Yolen; illustrated by Will Hillenbrand; musical arrangements by Adam Stemple ($20 including bonus CD; Candlewick Press)
♦ **Woof-Woof!** by Harriet Ziefert ($9; Blue Apple)
♦ **Baby Days: A Quilt of Rhymes and Pictures** by Belinda Downes ($15, Candlewick Press)
♦ **Goodnight Kisses** by Barney Saltzberg ($9, Red Wagon/Harcout)
♦ **Gossie & Friends** by Olivier Dunrea ($12; Houghton Mifflin)
♦ **Carry Me!** by Rosemary Wells ($16; Hyperion Books for Children)
♦ **Hug, Hug, Hug!; Num, Num, Num!** by Emily Jenkins; illustrated by Tomek Bogacki ($6 each; Farrar, Straus and Giroux)
♦ **Whose Toes Are Those?; Whose Knees Are These?** by Jabari Asim; illustrated by LeUyen Pham ($7 each; Little, Brown)
♦ **Where Is My Friend?** by Simms Taback ($8, Blue Apple)
♦ **Do Lions Live on Lily Pads?** by Melanie Walsh ($15; Houghton Mifflin)
♦ **Hickory Dickory Dock** by Margaret Barritt; illustrated by Jacqueline East ($8; Hand Print)

Mom Tip!

"In the car, I make sure my daughter has a book that I'm familiar with. When she wants me to play, I can tell her to flip to find a certain picture."

◆ **Jack and Jill** by R.A. Herman; illustrated by Olga and Aleksey Ivanov ($8 each; Handprint Books)

◆ **Numbers** by Michael Blake ($6; Candlewick Press)

◆ **Colors** by SAMI ($9; Blue Apple Books)

◆ **Cosy Cuddlers** by Jo Lodge ($8; Trafalgar)

◆ **Twinkle, Twinkle, Little Star** by Rosemary Wells ($7; Scholastic)

◆ **Baby Cakes** by Karma Wilson; illustrated by Sam Williams ($8; Little Simon)

◆ **Colors; Numbers** by Sara Anderson ($8 each; Hand Print)

◆ **Peek-a-Boo Who?** by Simms Taback ($9; Blue Apple Books)

◆ **Clip-Clop** by Nicola Smee ($13; Boxer Books)

◆ **Boats; Planes; Trucks; Trains** by Byron Barton ($13 each; HarperCollins)

◆ **My First Taggies Book: The Itsy-Bitsy Spider** ($7; Cartwheel/Scholastic)

◆ **Big Little** by SAMI ($9; Blue Apple)

◆ **Little Bunny; Little Butterfly** by Klaartje van der Put ($7 each; Chronicle)

18 MONTHS TO 3 YEARS:

◆ **Cheep! Cheep!** by Julie Stiegemeyer; illustrated by Carol Baicker-McKee ($10; Bloomsbury Children's Books)

◆ **Good Boy, Fergus!** by David Shannon ($16; Blue Sky/Scholastic)

◆ **Fast Food** by Saxton Freyman ($13; Levine/Scholastic)

◆ **Overboard!** by Sarah Weeks; illustrated by Sam Williams ($14; Harcourt)

◆ **There Is a Flower at the Tip of My Nose Smelling Me** by Alice Walker; illustrated by Stefano Vitale ($17; HarperCollins)

◆ **Walk On!** by Marla Frazee ($16; Harcourt)

◆ **"Fire, Fire!" Said Mrs. McGuire** by Bill Martin, Jr; illustrated by Vladimir Radunsky ($16; Harcourt)

◆ **Funny Face** by Nicola Smee ($9; Bloomsbury)

◆ **Up Above and Down Below** by Sue Redding ($15; Chronicle)

◆ **What Do Wheels Do All Day?** by April Jones Prince; illustrated by Giles Laroche ($16; Houghton Mifflin)

◆ **Hello Twins** by Charlotte Boake ($16; Candlewick Press)

◆ **How To Be** by Lisa Brown ($16; HarperCollins)

◆ **I Went Walking/Sali de Paseo** by Sue Williams; illustrated by Julie Vivas ($11; Harcourt)

◆ **So Sleepy Story** by Uri Shulevitz ($16; Farrar, Straus and Giroux)

◆ **Sleepyhead** by Karma Wilson; illustrated by John Segal ($16; McElderry/Simon & Schuster)

◆ **The Toolbox** by Anne and Harlow Rockwell ($7; Walker)

◆ **Mrs. Fickle's Pickles** by Lori Ries; illustrated by Nancy Cote ($17; Boyds Mills)

◆ **Tugga-Tugga Tugboat** by Kevin Lewis; illustrated by Danile Kirk ($16; Hyperion)

◆ **One Naked Baby** by Maggie Smith ($16; Knopf)

◆ **Pip & Squeak** by Ian Schoenherr ($17; Greenwillow)

◆ **Who Is Driving?** by Leo Timmers ($13; Bloomsbury)

◆ **Hurry! Hurry!** by Eve Bunting; illustrated by Jeff Mack ($16; Harcourt)

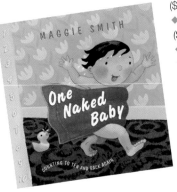

197

CLASSICS

In addition to the hundreds of wonderful new books that hit the shelves each year, there are some children's books (and authors) with timeless appeal. Some we especially love:

BOOKS

◆ **Goodnight, Moon** by Margaret Wise Brown and Clement Hurd
◆ **Guess How Much I Love You** by Sam McBratney
◆ **Brown Bear, Brown Bear, What Do You See?** by Bill Martin Jr. and Eric Carle
◆ **The Snowy Day** by Ezra Jack Keats
◆ **Harold and the Purple Crayon** by Crockett Johnson
◆ **Jamberry** by Bruce Degan
◆ **If You Give a Mouse a Cookie** by Laura Joffe Numeroff and Felicia Bonds

AUTHORS

◆ Lucy Cousins (author of the Maisy the Mouse books)
◆ Janet and Allan Ahlberg
◆ Eric Carle
◆ Shirley Hughes
◆ Sandra Boynton (author of fun rhyming books like **Barnyard Dance** and **Pajama Time**)
◆ Audrey Wood
◆ Helen Oxenbury
◆ Jan Brett
◆ Leo Lionni
◆ Rosemary Wells
◆ Richard Scarry
◆ Dr. Seuss

EDITORS' FAVES

Babies and toddlers love to read their favorite books again and again, and again. Here, some titles that *Parenting* magazine's editors enjoyed reading day after day, night after night, to their own kids:

Good Night, Gorilla by Peggy Rathmann (Putnam Juvenile) "Few words, so you supply your own narrative. Great for ni-night time."

The Going To Bed Book by Sandra Boynton (Little Simon) "Great read-aloud, nice rhythms and rhymes, and the ending ('and rock, and rock, and rock…to…sleep'), read in a whisper, is sleep-inducing."

The Cat in the Hat Comes Back by Dr. Seuss (Random House Books for Young Readers) "Underrated (and superior) sequel to *Cat in Hat.* Kids love the little tiny cats in the Hat Cat's hat. Secretly it's an alphabet book, but it's mostly just fun."

Big Red Barn by Margaret Wise Brown and Felicia Bond (HarperFestival) "We had this as a board book. Lots of little animals to look at and make sounds. Very simple text. They all go to sleep at the end, so it's a great bedtime book. Illustrations don't stray into cloying."

Where Did Josie Go? by Helen Elizabeth Buckley, Jan Ormerod (HarperCollins) "Both of my girls loved this. I sang it like it was a song."

10 Minutes Till Bedtime by Peggy Rathmann (Putnam Juvenile) "No words except the father saying '10 minutes 'till bedtime.' Endless things to look at and point out. At the end the little boy is exhausted and in bed, so it is a help in that way."

The Merry Chase by Clement Hurd (Chronicle Books) "My son loved the vivid drawings as well as the upbeat rhythm of the language."

Good Night, Baby! by DK Publishing (DK Preschool) "My ob/gyn gave this little board book to me at my six-week post-partum checkup, and it's been one of my son's favorites from the beginning— lots of up-close face shots, which babies love, and it showed my son what a bedtime routine is."

Caterpillar's Wish by Mary Elizabeth Murphy (DK Preschool) "About a caterpillar who wishes for wings, so she could join her flying friends. Then she metamorphoses. My daughter never got tired of that amazing last page when Caterpillar gets enormous, colorful wings. I liked the book as well, because although it's a paperback, the paper is extra-thick and tear-resistant."

Baby Duck and the Cozy Blanket by Amy Hest, Jill Barton (Candlewick Press) "We still read it all the time. The pages have lots of textures for kids to explore, and they love the story of how Baby Duck reluctantly lets her mom wash her dirty blanket, then is delighted with how clean the blanket turns out. I've even brought it to Genie's preschool to read aloud when I'm Shabbat Mom."

Go, Dog, Go! by P.D. Eastman (Random House/Beginner) "Lots of opportunity for me to make all the funny voices I can muster."

One Morning in Maine by Robert McCloskey (Puffin) "Even though it's kind of long, both kids sit still for it, and I NEVER get tired of looking at Robert McCloskey's drawings."

Moo, Baa, La La La by Sandra Boynton (Simon & Schuster Childrens Books) "Great singsongy rhythm and cute pix."

The Very Hungry Caterpillar by Eric Carle (Philomel) "My kids loved sticking their little fingers in the leaf holes."

My Very First Mother Goose by Iona Opie, Rosemary Wells (Candlewick Press) "Beautiful pix and a comprehensive collection including some lyrical rarities."

YOUR BABY HAS BEEN LISTENING to tunes since before she was born: Whatever you blasted in the car, relaxed with in the evenings, and exercised to in the gym, your child could hear from the second trimester on. She may even show a liking for some of those songs now, if she heard them often enough. But babies have innate preferences for certain types of sounds, and these can help you select the music your child listens to.

◆ **Rhythmic sounds** Because they remind them of the noises of the womb (your heartbeat, the whooshing of blood through your veins), babies love the ticking of a clock or the whirring of a fan and similar sounds. A recording of nature sounds may be all a newborn needs to settle down to sleep.

◆ **Slow, lilting music** Lullabies truly are calming.

◆ **The human voice** Infants love to hear people sing—especially Mom—so recordings by female singers may be especially appealing to them.

This isn't to say that the only thing babies like to listen to are women singing "Rock-a-Bye Baby." The popularity of CDs made just for kids, by musicians who cater to kids, is testament to that. The best way to choose music for your child is to listen to it together and find tunes that you both like. And don't feel pressured to expose her to classical music at every turn: The connection between Mozart and brainpower has been grossly overhyped. That said, many of the moms in our survey mentioned that they'd bought CDs of classical music, as well as lullabies, for their babies to listen to (many especially loved Baby Einstein CDs and DVDs)—and the tunes were enjoyed by all. The bottom line: Stick to music you can tolerate and that your baby responds to.

PARENTING PICKS: CDS

Jazz Baby, Sessions 1-3 Various artists ($10 each CD; Casablanca Kids, casablancakids.com)

Color Wheel Cartwheel Laura Freeman ($16 CD; Green Kid Music, greenkid.com)

Nicky's Jazz Lullabies ($18; Dominick Media, nickythejazzcat.com)

Bingo: Songs for Children in English with Brazilian and Caribbean Rhythms ($18; Soundbrush, forteddistri-bution.com)

Reggae Playground ($15; Putumayo, putumayo.com)

Quiet Time Raffi ($13; Rounder)

Alphabet Jam Cathy Bollinger ($16; Rivanna Music)

Baby Loves Jazz Go Baby Go ($13; Verve)

Children Are The Sunshine Asheba ($15; COV Productions, asheba.net)

Baby Love: Play Time ($7; Music For Little People)

You Are My Little Bird Elizabeth Mitchell ($12, Smith-sonian Folkways, folkways.si.edu/index.html)

Jack's Big Music Show, Season 1 ($13; Nick Records, Nickshop.com)

Rockin' in the Forest With Farmer Jason ($17; Kid Rhino)

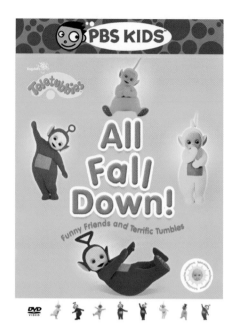

TUBE-TIME FOR KIDS is a controversial issue. Experts warn against using a video as a babysitter or setting a baby in front of a so-called "educational" DVD in order to jump-start her brain development. Babies learn best by one-on-one interaction with Mom, Dad, siblings, and others, not by passively watching TV. To that end, the American Academy of Pediatrics recommends that:

◆ **children under the age of 2** watch no television at all (even so-called educational videos and DVDS)

◆ **kids 2 and over** be limited to no more than two hours per day of screen time (including the computer screen).

Even so, plenty of DVDs are marketed to babies and toddlers, and, if used judiciously, some of them can be part of a child's total learning experience (and give you a break, too—after all, a little screen time is better than a mom who's at her wit's end!)

Just keep it short and when you can, watch with your child and comment on what's on the screen, even if you're folding laundry or stirring the pasta sauce at the same time. Name the objects on the screen, clap along to the music, and so forth.

THE BEST DVDS FOR BABIES:

◆ **Feature simple, familiar images.** What a baby sees on the screen should be no more complicated than what she sees in a board book: The only difference is she might see the puppy in action (barking) or the stacking cups fall down.

◆ **Are divided into short segments.** That is, a song followed by a simple game, for example, so you can watch a little bit here, a little bit there.

◆ **Have baby-friendly soundtracks.** Avoid videos with loud, raucous music and sound effects.

◆ **Don't try too hard to teach.** Even if a baby video claims to be educational, with classic music and other brainy elements, the presentation should be sweet and simple.

PARENTING PICKS: DVDS (BIRTH TO 18 MONTHS)

◆ **Make a Wish, Little Fish** ($13; Music for Little People)
◆ **Baby Tata** ($20; babytata.com)
◆ **Fun Baby** ($20; Calm Baby)
◆ **Classical Baby** ($27 for three-disc set; HBO)
◆ **Baby Wordsworth** ($20; Baby Einstein)
◆ **The Baby Society** ($20; the babysociety.com)
◆ **Beginning Together** ($15; Sesame Workshop/ Sony Wonder)

◆ **Baby Inklings: Alphabet Discovery** ($15; VisionTrek Studios)
◆ **Baby Songbird; Smarty Symphony** ($15; babysongbird.com)
◆ **Teletubbies: All Fall Down!** ($15; Paramount)
◆ **Boohbah: Building Blocks** ($15, PBS Kids/Paramount)
◆ **Meet the Colors** ($15; Preschool Prep Company, preschoolprepco.com)
◆ **Yoga Ma Baby Ga** ($25; downdogproductions.com)

THE BEST DVDS FOR TODDLERS:

◆ **Tell very simple stories.** Kids this age can't follow complicated plots, nor will they "get" the humor in films made for older kids.

◆ **Feature interactive games and songs.** As with babies, you want to avoid passive watching; look for DVDs that ask your child to sing along or play along.

◆ **Get them moving.** You don't want your small-fry to grow up to be a couch potato: DVDs that encourage kids to mimic the movements of the characters are ideal.

◆ **Teach about the world.** Forget hoity-toity lessons about Mozart and Picasso (which isn't to say that a classical soundtrack is a bad thing; it just shouldn't be the point): Opt for DVDs about things your child encounters in her day-to-day life, like animals, vehicles, the grocery store.

◆ **Enhance their experience with books.** It's sometimes fun to see your favorite characters from the pages of a book come to life on screen. The best movie versions of toddler tomes stick to the script.

PARENTING PICKS: DVDS
(18 MONTHS TO 3 YEARS)

◆ **The Backyardigans: The Snow Fort**
($14; Nickelodeon)

◆ **Hi! I'm Todd** ($13; HIT Entertainment)

◆ **Goodnight Moon and Other Sleepytime Tales**
($13; HBO)

◆ **Eebee's Adventures: Figuring Things Out!**
($15; Sony Wonder)

◀ EEBEE'S ADVENTURES: FIGURING THINGS OUT! ($15)

◆ **AthleticBaby: Basketball**
($17; athleticBaby.com)
◆ **Eyecandy: Can You See It?**
($20; braincandykids.com)
◆ **The Busy Little Engine** ($16; Squirrel
Tracks, busylittleengine.com)
◆ **Elmo's World; Pets** ($13; Sony Wonder/
Sesame Workshop)
◆ **Monkeydoos: Things that Go!**
($15; Mazzarella Media)
◆ **Little Robots: Big Adventures**
($15; Warner Bros.)
◆ **Barney: Let's Make Music** ($20; HIT
Entertainment/20th Century Fox Home Entertainment)
◆ **Little Playdates, Vol. 2: Little Adventurers**
($15 DVD, $18 DVD/CD; Three Coin Productions,
littleplaydates.com)
◆ **Way to Go, Juno!** ($20; junobaby.com)

12

STORAGE

THE AMOUNT OF STUFF you'll accumulate for your baby during his first two years will no doubt be mind-boggling: diapers, wipes, toiletries; T-shirts, sleepers, socks, and booties; rattles, board books, toys, and more toys.... Where do you keep it all, so that stuff is both handy and yet not so "out there" that it creates clutter? And how do you make sure that any potentially dangerous items are put away where curious little fingers can't reach them?

There are as many different storage solutions as there are types of baby gear and products. Here are some of our mom-testers' favorites, along with suggestions as to what goes where.

BOXES AND BINS

THESE COME IN A MULTITUDE OF SHAPES, varieties, sizes, and styles, made of wicker (often with decorative fabric liners), canvas, brightly-colored plastic, faux leather, or wire or metal with painted or shiny finishes. Many fit on the shelves of a changing table and are a great way to keep stacks of diapers neat and contained. Others make terrific under-bed storage for toys and books, especially in bedrooms too small for lots of shelving.

Canvas totes or baskets with handles are great for storing anything that needs to be portable—like toys you might want to move from one part of the home to another. (And toddlers love to carry things around; smaller-handled baskets will provide loads of entertainment once your child is walking.)

ROLLING BOXES AND BINS Anything on casters makes clean-up easy: Just roll the container from mess to mess, then wheel it into a corner or out-of-sight.

◄ ROLLAWAY MESS: CASTERS ON STORAGE TUBS ARE AN ADDED BONUS.

208

POP-UP BINS Also a great choice for large toys and stuffed animals, these can be pressed down flat when not needed, then can spring into service to hold laundry, stray playthings, or anything else that needs to be gathered up and stashed away. One great option: **Land of Nod's** pop-up bins, which come in lots of colors and retail for $8 to $10 each (landofnod.com). And **Bongo Bags** ($13; itoy-boxes.com) are great for storing long, narrow items.

▲ POP-UP BINS, LIKE THESE FROM LAND OF NOD ($8-$10), CAN CREATE ORDER IN EVERY ROOM OF THE HOUSE.

GIZMOS & GADGETS

If you spend a lot of time in your car with your baby in tow, the seats and floor can get quickly overrun with Cheerios, toys, books, and the like. Here are two organizers designed for your car that our mom-testers loved:
The Safe Fit Back Seat Storage With Seat Protector slips under your child's car seat and keeps your upholstery clean, and the extra pockets and detachable box keep toys close and contained ($25; Blue Ridge).
The Kids Activity Tray (left) wraps around your child's car seat to form a surface for drawing or coloring and folds up into a mini-briefcase when you're not using it ($20; Case Logic). One of our mom-testers said, "My son loves having a play area on his car seat! The side pockets hold all his art supplies."

STURDY STACKABLE BINS Land of Nod's Wooden Storage-Palooza Bins can eliminate lots of clutter and look grown-up enough for a living room. Their slanted openings make them easy for kids to access ($149; landofnod.com).

LABELED BOXES These come in all shapes and sizes, with lids and without, and in a variety of materials, from canvas to fabric-covered cardboard. They're great for stashing little things that are easily lost, like teensy manicure scissors and spare pacifiers, as well as those mementos and photographs you haven't had time to stick in the scrapbook.

▲ LAND OF NOD'S STOR-AGE-PALOOZA BINS ($149) ARE CLASSIC ENOUGH THAT YOUR CHILD CAN USE THEM FOR YEARS.

CANVAS BOXES WITH HANDLES In different sizes, they're useful for everything from laundry to diaper-changing essentials to toys. **Babystyle's Storage Boxes** come in a number of sizes and two patterns: striped or denim ($14–$38; babystyle.com).

▲ YOU CAN COORDINATE ALL OF YOUR NURSERY STORAGE WITH BABYSTYLE'S STORAGE BOXES ($14–$38).

CLEAR PLASTIC BOXES Nothing beats a container you can see through for making it easy to find stuff. Often called "lookers" boxes, you can find these in all sizes and colors. They're especially useful if you have more than one child and are storing clothes until they're ready to be handed down. Check out **The Container Store** (containerstore.com) for clear boxes in a range of sizes, as well as a huge selection of other items for storage and organization.

LARGE, SHALLOW CANVAS BOXES WITH LIDS that fit under the crib are perfect for storing out-of-season and next-size-up baby duds, as well as extra crib linens, blankets, and other items. The lids are key: They'll keep dust off that hand-knit sweater from Gran.

▲ LOOKERS NESTED BOXES ($30; CONTAINER-STORE.COM) COME IN SETS OF SIX, IN EITHER CLEAR OR RAIN-BOW COLORS.

▶ POTTERY BARN KIDS LIDDED CANVAS BOXES ($45) COME WITH DIVIDER INSERTS. FOR EVEN MORE ORGANIZATION!

211

TOY CHESTS While not the most organized way to store playthings (stuff just gets tossed in and jumbled about), you might like the look of a classic toy chest in your child's room—and options abound, from hard plastic models to hand-painted, heirloom quality pieces of art. Some we like: **Step 2**'s innovative plastic-and-fabric toy box, which features a panel of fabric with storage pockets across the front (about $60 at step2.com); **Offi's wooden roll-top bench,** which doubles as seating ($300); **Guidecraft**'s wooden toy box ($160; guidecraft.com); and the **Mission Design Toy Box** ($139.99; littletikes.com), which has a safety hinge and openings under the lid to keep from pinching little fingers.

Besides choosing a style that fits in with your décor, it's important to keep a few safety issues in mind, especially if you're buying a used chest from a yard sale or second-hand store: In 2001, the Consumer Product Safety Commission issued a warning about chests with free-falling lids when several children were killed or injured while reaching into a toy chest. Make sure the toy chest you buy has a lid that stays open. (If you have your heart set on one that doesn't, you can install a lid support that will hold the lid open in any position; check it frequently to make sure it works properly.) Also, make sure the chest has openings that allow air to flow in; children have suffocated after being trapped in toy chests.

▲ OFFI'S ROLL-TOP WOODEN BENCH ($300) LOOKS GREAT, HIDES THE MESS, AND ADDS EXTRA SEATING.

▶ GUIDECRAFT ALSO MAKES TOY BOXES PAINTED WITH LOGOS OF MAJOR LEAGUE BASEBALL TEAMS ($160), FOR LITTLE SPORTS FANS.

▲ IF YOU FIND YOURSELF TRIPPING OVER STUFFED ANIMALS, THE BOON ANIMAL BAG DOES DOUBLE DUTY AS STORAGE SACK AND SOFT SEAT, ALL ZIPPED UP IN A FUZZY, KID-FRIENDLY DESIGN. THEY'RE BETWEEN $60 AND $100, DEPENDING ON THE STYLE (BOONINC.COM).

▲ AN UPDATE ON OVER-DOOR SHOE POCKETS, IKEA'S HANGING ORGANIZERS ($4 TO $15) COME IN A VARIETY OF SHAPES, FROM ROCKETS TO DRAGONS TO PLAIN ROUND.

SHOE HOLDERS Those designed to hang on the inside of a closet door, with clear vinyl pockets, can be a neat, space-saving solution for storing all sorts of little items, from your baby's socks, T-shirts, and small toys, to tubes of diaper cream, teensy hair brushes, nail scissors, and more. You also can easily organize baby things in shoe cubbies, like the **12 Cube Organizer by Stacks and Stacks** ($60; stacksandstacks.com).

To keep all of those little wardrobe items organized, our mom-testers like the canvas **Koala Baby Closet Organizer** ($25, Babies 'R' Us).

▲ OVER-DOOR SHOE ORGANIZERS, LIKE THIS ONE FROM STACKS AND STACKS ($22), HOLD EVERYTHING FROM STUFFED ANIMALS TO DVDS—AND EVEN SHOES!

SHELVING

EVEN WITH STORAGE BINS AND BOXES galore, there rarely seems to be enough space for everything. That's where shelving comes in!

WALL-MOUNTED SHELVING The area above the changing table can be dead space—or it can be the perfect spot to secure a shelf or two to hold the necessities of diaper changes, including toys to distract your little wiggler and decorative containers for rash cream and such. Mounting a shelf above the changing table is an especially good idea if your changing table doesn't have open shelving.

▲ WHEN MOUNTED CLOSE TOGETHER ON THE WALL, LAND OF NOD'S TOP SHELF SHELVES ($39) CAN DOUBLE AS BOOKENDS.

214

FREE-STANDING SHELVING You'll want to make sure anything you put in your child's room is tip-proof and not too tall (because once they can stand, most kids like to climb). But there are a number of great storage shelves that do double duty as room dividers. One that our mom-testers liked is the **Arch Pass-Thru Storage Shelf** ($170; Guidecraft). Storage on

▲ GUIDECRAFT'S ARCH PASS-THRU STORAGE SHELF ($170) COMES WITH HEAVY-DUTY CASTERS, SO IT CAN BE MOVED AROUND THE NURSERY IF NECESSARY.

two sides makes this ideal for dividing a shared room with a play area on either side. Target has several very reasonably priced kids' shelving alternatives: Its **Storage Shelf with Bins** ($60) comes with 12 colorful tilted containers (in your choice of palette) for toys of every shape and size. The store also has bookcases with colorful bins in different configurations ($70–$100).

Another modern-looking option from Design Within Reach is **Cubitec Shelving** ($198 for a kit; each kit makes 6 cubes; dwr.com). These polypropelene panels come in several colors as well as translucent, and can be configured however you like, making them very versatile. Also from Design Within Reach, **Cubits** have the option of adding doors ($178 for a kit; each kit can make up to four cubes).

▼ CUBITS SHELVING FROM DESIGN WITHIN REACH ($178) CAN BE ASSEMBLED IN NUMEROUS CONFIGURATIONS.

13 THE SHOPPING GUIDE

YOU MAY WANT TO buy certain items at a local juvenile store to save shipping charges, or to have a convenient place to return and repair things. If there isn't a good baby store nearby, or if you're looking to explore more options, here are some of moms' favorite resources.

NATIONAL RETAILERS

Any of the following mass merchants would be a good place to cross a lot of items off of your list:

◆ BABIES 'R' US
Babiesrus.com
Great selection of everything you need for a baby, on display for you to try out. The prices are good, though this is not the place to go for an heirloom quilt. Baby registry.

◆ BUY BUY BABY
Buybuybaby.com
Wide and deep variety of baby gear in all price points—from cribs and gliders to breast pumps, bouncer seats, and every imaginable accessory. Plus all of the small stuff, such as pacifiers, breast milk storage bags, diaper cream, etc. Baby registry.

◆ KMART
Kmart.com
Besides the small stuff, has many inexpensive options for big-ticket items like cribs and high chairs.

◆ THE RIGHT START
Rightstart.com
A very attractive, well-edited selection of everything you'll need, short of furniture (no cribs, changing tables, etc.). Baby registry.

217

◆ TARGET

Target.com

Proprietary brands such as Amy Coe for great-looking bedding, clothes, and room accessories and Circo for baby wardrobe basics, bath towels, and the like. Also carries many other brands, and a variety of furniture and gear, though there's not as wide a selection as you'd find at a juvenile retailer. The website makes it easy to search by feature—and parent reviews can be very useful.

◆ WALMART

Walmart.com

Good values, though far less variety than you'd find at a baby-only retailer.

SPECIALTY RETAILERS

These national retailers are super resources for some (though not all) of the items on your list.

◆ CHILDREN'S PLACE

Childrensplace.com

Stylish kids' clothing, terrific sales.

◆ THE CONTAINER STORE

Containerstore.com

Nice-looking storage solutions for every room of the house.

◆ BABYGAP

babygap.com

Clothing for boys and girls from the minute they're born until they're finishing up pre-school (at which point it's time for GapKids). Excellent sales, and big benefits from getting a Gap (or Old Navy—Gap Inc. operates both chains) credit card.

◆ H & M

Hm.com (to locate stores only—not a shopping site)

Super style, wonderful cottons, and exceptionally good prices if there's a store near you. Only some of the H&M stores carry baby and children's clothes.

◆ IKEA

Ikea.com (to locate stores; many items can only be purchased in-store)

Cheap, very basic, but well-designed cribs and changing tables, plus cool-looking little-kid furnishings (chairs, tables, organizing gear, etc.).

◀ IKEA'S MAMMUT FURNITURE LINE IS FULL OF WHIMSICAL PIECES LIKE THIS DRESSER ($114).

◆ OLD NAVY
oldnavy.com
Well-priced clothing for babies, toddlers, and bigger kids that is slightly less expensive than items from sister company, the Gap. The first Tuesday of every month is sale day.

◆ STRIDE RITE
striderite.com
A wide selection of expertly engineered shoes for babies and children, and Certified Fit Specialists in stores make sure that the shoes fit.

CATALOGS AND E-TAILERS

These e-tailers (some of which have catalogs as well) have especially good selections:

◆ AMAZON
amazon.com
With a wider selection of products than other e-tailers, this can be your one-stop cybershop for everything from furniture to toys. Consumer ratings and reviews are particularly helpful. Baby registry.

◆ BABYCENTER
Babycenter.com
Helpful consumer reviews, a wide variety of well-chosen products, and easy navigation. Baby registry.

◆ BABY STYLE
Babystyle.com
Exclusive, well-designed nursery décor and clothing that's also reasonably priced. Good rewards program (spend a few hundred dollars and get $10 plus special discounts and other incentives to keep spending). Baby registry.

◆ GIGGLE
egiggle.com
Sleek, stylish (and pricey) gear, including bouncy seats, diaper bags, and furniture, that will coordinate with modern décor.

◆ HANNA ANDERSSON
Hannaandersson.com
Swedish cotton separates, one-piece rompers, and more in appealing patterns that hold up wash after wash (and child after child!).

◆ LAND OF NOD
Landofnod.com
Owned by Crate & Barrel, Land of Nod has opened a handful of stores, but for now, the catalog and website are still the best places to find whimsically designed, well-made (and priced accordingly) nursery furniture and accessories. Check out the "nods and ends" clearance section.

▼ QUALITY AND COLOR: HANNA ANDERSSON "ZIPPER" ($28 TO $36).

◆ LANDS' END KIDS
Landsend.com
Sturdy, stylish, extremely well-priced outerwear, footwear, and all things fleece.

◆ MODERNTOTS
moderntots.com
Super-hip, expensive nursery furniture and accessories.

◆ ONE STEP AHEAD
Onestepahead.com
A thoughtful selection of health, safety, bath, and feeding products.

◆ PERFECTLY SAFE
perfectlysafe.stores.yahoo.net
Everything you'll need to childproof your home.

◆ POTTERY BARN KIDS
Potterybarnkids.com
Classic, well-made baby furniture (cribs, gliders, changing tables, storage solutions) and bedding.

◆ TRAVELING TIKES
Travelingtikes.com
Well-selected on-the-go merchandise (strollers, car seats, carriers, etc.).

▲ LANDS' END SNOWSUITS ARE WATERPROOF AND AFFORDABLE ($59.50).

◄ PINT-SIZE MOD FURNITURE FOR KIDS LIKE THE OEUF MINI LIBRARY ($560), IS AVAILABLE ON MODERNTOTS. COM.

GREEN RETAILERS

These sites feature environmentally-friendly products, from clothing and furniture to bath products. They all offer online shopping.

GREENHOME.COM
greenhome.com
Organic and recycled products for family and home.

HAPPYGREENBEE
happygreenbee.com
Mix and match clothing made from organic cotton.

NATURE'S CRIB
naturescrib.com
Organic baby clothes and bedding; natural baby-care products, furniture, wood toys.

OUR GREENHOUSE
ourgreenhouse.com
Organic baby clothes and bedding; bath products; toys, and furnishings.

BARGAIN HUNTING

Most of the sources listed in this chapter have clearance areas on their sites, so it's always a good idea to check these out for off-season merchandise or last season's designs at a deep discount. In addition, these sites are particularly easy to use and can help you land the best price on something once you've scoped out a particular model:

◆ STROLLERSFORLESS.COM
For the e-tailers with the best prices on all types of strollers.

◆ EPINIONS.COM
In the "Kids and Family" section, you can find consumer ratings and reviews as well as the best prices on a range of equipment and furniture, usually factoring in for shipping charges.

PARENTING.COM
We're finding great new products all the time. Check out "Our Daily Fave" (editors' picks), and other Mom-Tested products.

▶ GENDER NEUTRAL: HAPPYGREEN-BEE'S SEPARATES (FROM $10 TO $32 PER PIECE) WORK FOR BOTH GIRLS AND BOYS.

221

INDEX

Page numbers in **bold-face** refer to illustrations.

223

PHOTO CREDITS